PRAIS_
The Observer

"A powerful work with insights that, once applied, will help you lift your life to a completely new level."
—**ROBIN SHARMA,** #1 BESTSELLING AUTHOR OF *THE 5AM CLUB* AND *THE MONK WHO SOLD HIS FERRARI*

"In *The Observer*, Todd's concept of the 180-degree mindset aligns with my theory of every 'coin' having three sides—two sides and the edge. The more we see and learn and the more possibilities we explore, the smarter and more powerful we become. Todd's new book is, indeed, wisdom for the journey of life."
—**ROBERT KIYOSAKI,** AUTHOR OF THE INTERNATIONAL BESTSELLER *RICH DAD POOR DAD*

"In between stimulus and response lies *The Observer*. Todd Stottlemyre has written a poignant tale of success, wealth, and fame being darkened by a lack of purpose and fulfillment. Like Todd in real life, the fictional protagonist Kat appears to have it all. However, looks can be deceiving and life has a way of turning in the blink of an eye. With her world turned upside down, Kat discovers clarity through the wisdom and the guidance of her observer. This is a beautifully written book that at times hauntingly mirrors Todd's life and the challenges he has faced. In today's trying times, we all can use the wisdom of *The Observer* and in his writing, Todd has provided us with the path of discovery."

—GUY ADAMI, CNBC's FAST MONEY

"*The Observer* created a new way for me to see the world. This story of a hard-charging woman running a fashion company clearly illustrates how a simple change to your mindset can achieve untold results."

—HAL ELROD, INTERNATIONAL KEYNOTE SPEAKER
AND BESTSELLING AUTHOR OF
THE MIRACLE MORNING AND *THE MIRACLE EQUATION*

"*The Observer* is a well-written book that embodies the ups and downs and potential roadblocks in one's pursuit of not only success but happiness. Todd was an amazing teammate, and I was always impressed and intrigued with his desire to want to be more than just a MLB pitcher. He was one of the most insightful, thought-provoking teammates I ever had, and I always enjoyed his company. I am not surprised by his knowledge and ability to instruct and describe what it means to be great and how you comprise a process and mindset to achieve excellence. His all-in and no-nonsense approach to everything he does is refreshing in today's world."

—AL LEITER, FORMER MLB PITCHER
AND CURRENT MLB NETWORK ANALYST

"*The Observer* created a new way for me to see the world. This story clearly illustrates how a simple change to your mindset can achieve untold results."

—DAVE CANALES, SEATTLE SEAHAWKS
OFFENSIVE PASSING GAME COORDINATOR

"A major step forward in the study of achievement. Todd knocks the ball out of the park!"

—CHRIS WIDENER, *NEW YORK TIMES*
AND *WALL STREET JOURNAL* BESTSELLING AUTHOR OF
THE ANGEL INSIDE

"Todd has done a masterful job completing the picture of achieving peak performance by taking mindset, mindfulness, and intentionality and applying it to maximize talent, opportunity, and goals. This book is practical in its application and game changing in revealing a holistic revelation of pursuing and achieving peak performance."

—PATRICK VAN DEN BOSSCHE, PRESIDENT,
REALTY EXECUTIVES INTERNATIONAL

"Todd Stottlemyre is a rarity of epic proportions as a human, coach, and high-performer. A master of achievement and personal performance who can duplicate it with others. All who work with him out-perform, out-earn, and outlast their competition and even their own limited beliefs. Meeting him early in my entrepreneurial career was the gift that completely changed my trajectory and running with his mentorship compressed time for my success. Thank you, Todd, for evolving my human capacities and the world's. You are the true master, and if it's written by Todd, it's a read I will bury my mind in."

—DANELLE DELGADO,
BUSINESS AND BRAND STRATEGIST

"*The Observer* is a powerful story about faith, resilience, habits, and mindset. Todd is someone who has been in the heat of the battle on a worldwide stage. He has fought and battled from the pitcher's mound and then reinvented himself as an entrepreneur, speaker, and author using the same powerful principles and habits that helped him have a successful MLB career. Learn from Todd, he has lived what he teaches. Thank you, Todd, for wanting to make us all better!"

—**KYLE WILSON,** STRATEGIST, MARKETER, FOUNDER OF JIM ROHN INTERNATIONAL

"3-time World-Champion, Entrepreneur, Success Coach, Author and Orator Todd Stottlemyre is impacting lives globally. His success principles are very well-delivered in an easy-to-read story form in *The Observer*. Todd's coaching through this book will get you to advance your life financially, mentally and emotionally."

—**DANNY BAE,** GPS CO-FOUNDER AND CHAIRMAN

The Observer

*A Modern Fable on Mastering
Your Thoughts & Emotions*

Todd Stottlemyre

Made for Success
PUBLISHING

Made for Success Publishing
P.O. Box 1775 Issaquah, WA 98027
www.MadeForSuccessPublishing.com

Distributed by Made for Success Publishing

First Printing

Library of Congress Cataloging-in-Publication data

Stottlemyre, Todd
     The Observer: A Modern Fable on Mastering Your Thoughts &
     Emotions
     p. cm.
LCCN: 2020947270
ISBN: 978-1-64146-534-2 (*Paperback*)
ISBN: 978-1-64146-555-7 (*eBook*)
ISBN: 978-1-64146-556-4 (*Audiobook*)

For further information contact Made for Success Publishing
+14255266480 or email service@madeforsuccess.net
Printed in the United States of America

ONE

A SHARP YELL pierced the pre-dawn stillness of the mountain lake, followed by a splash. She knew that a quick out-push of air would counteract the involuntary gasp when her body plunged into frigid water, keeping her from accidentally inhaling water. Nothing like a polar plunge to shock her system into high alert. Kicking hard, she did a round of breaststrokes before her body became too numb, and then scrambled up the ladder onto the pier. Quickly drying her nude body off with the towel she had left there, she slipped into stylish sweats and tennis shoes.

The upscale sports clothes were from her own store, Ace-It Athletics. It was a small chain of stores in Toronto she had launched four years previously, with resounding success. As she jogged back uphill to her cabin, plans for opening the next store, the first in Montreal, churned in her mind. Once inside, she finished the morning exercise routine with pushups, sit-ups, weights, and spinning. It was less extensive than the gym routine she did every morning after leaving home at 4:30 a.m., but the cabin was small. The polar plunge, she surmised, made up for the lack.

Kat—Katerina Von Slyke—was 38 years old and hitting her peak. Kat was her preferred name, as it was more efficient, and efficiency is what drove her business. She kept her lean 5-foot, 8-inch frame toned and muscular through an effective, demanding, and relentless daily workout. She ran her 16-store business of high-end sports clothes and accessories in an equally effectual way, expecting consistent top-level performance from her employees. Kat was relentlessly persistent in pursuit of success. Her father, Vince Von Slyke, was her role model in many ways. He had been a star pitcher for the Toronto Blue Jays baseball team and was now the general manager. She saw him as the master of living a championship life, one whose teachings had guided her to success.

Her demanding morning routine followed her father's model for "The Championship Hour." "How you start the day shapes the rest of the day, week, year, and your entire life. In this critical hour, you work on yourself and prepare for winning. It sets the pattern for a peak performance lifestyle and molds you into a champion," he had said. Kat was determined to win and attain high-level success, and she believed her persistence would propel her to reach the greatest version of herself.

Kat knew that all obstacles to the championship life must be overcome or removed. She was just not sure which category fit her ex-husband Bryce.

He was a nice enough guy but lacked drive or ambition. His values simply didn't fit with her peak performance lifestyle. When things became conflicted in their relationship, he wanted to work on the marriage. He tried several approaches to save it, from couple's therapy to self-help fix-it remedies. Kat resented the time this took away from her business and found she couldn't focus on his attempted solutions. Bryce said she was unwilling to put in the work to save their marriage.

It hurt when he left, and, as difficult as it was to admit, she still felt it. The way she saw it, the breakup of their marriage was a failure, something she found hard to take. Now Bryce had become a symbol of failures, both hers and his. He gave up and left when the going got rough, unable to accept the sacrifices necessary to achieve her ambitions. So, she had to let something important go—which was *not* her M.O.—and the loss still annoyingly gnawed away at her.

Her driven lifestyle and work ethic had propelled her to an $8 million per year income, an expensive high-rise condo in Heathrow Towers in the exclusive Forest Hills neighborhood of Toronto, and a secluded cabin on Vermillion Lake near Banff. She loved the rustic cabin; it was her refuge and weekend escape for unwinding. Most of the time, she came alone, hoping the quiet would restore her.

This was her favorite time of year at Banff, the late spring when the mountain lakes were thawing, the air yet still crisp and cold. Vermillion Lake was at the edge of the Banff townsite; her cabin was tucked into a cove with no nearby houses. Vermillion was one of the earliest lakes to thaw, making it the perfect time and place for doing a polar plunge. As the summer came, the lake took on the famous turquoise blue-green color that drew visitors from around the world. Silt from melting glaciers entering the lake and reflecting sunlight created the magnificent colors.

During the summer, she brought her 14-year-old son Sky to the cabin. It was a favorite vacation for them both, full of water sports, hiking, and bird-watching. Sky was a bright light in Kat's life, always cheerful and supportive of her work. He attended high school at the Lawrence Park Collegiate Institute, a highly regarded college prep school with a brick exterior that spoke of tradition and prestige. She made a point of always attending his baseball games. He was quickly gaining skill and becoming a first-rate pitcher, hoping to follow in his grandfather's footsteps. During school days, a limo picked Sky up and took him the 8 km distance from the condo to school, allowing Kat to get to the office earlier.

Sunday evening was fast approaching, and Kat still felt keyed up. Despite the placid setting and soothing stillness, she could not unwind. She finished the text message she was working on, hit send, and set the phone aside. Putting on jogging shoes, she set out for a 5-mile loop that she frequently took following the lake's curved shoreline. The temperature hovered in the upper 40s, and clouds hung low over the mountains. Few other hikers would be out today, so she set a gruesome pace and tried to work off her tension. The physical exertion and later packing for the flight home kept her distracted; it was as close as she got to being relaxed.

Kat boarded her private jet at the airport near Banff in the evening. She always chose to fly at night so she could sleep on the plane. This way, she did not waste valuable time and could hit the ground running on Monday when she returned to Toronto. This particular night, however, she had trouble falling asleep, her mind unable to disengage with planning the launch of her new store just two weeks out. She ran through the items for the early morning staff meeting, making mental notes about what she wanted each employee to accomplish. She was a bit apprehensive about the new store's launch budget. No matter how she crunched the numbers, it looked like the venture was under-funded. In the staff meeting, she would get the latest figures. *They better be good*, she thought.

Monday morning, after landing at 4:30 a.m., she had her limo driver take her to the gym for her usual morning workout. He waited in the parking lot and then drove her to the condo, where she took a quick shower, dressed for work, and grabbed a power shake for breakfast. Sky was up, having his usual two eggs and whole-wheat toast. He was a fantastic cook and enjoyed preparing meals for his mom, who really detested cooking.

"Hi, Mom, good weekend?" Sky asked.

"Not the best, but good. Especially the polar plunge. The lake was almost clear of ice, and the water cold enough to put me in hypothermia in less than five minutes," Kat replied.

"Bet that woke you up for sure. It's pretty cold even in the summer when I like to swim."

"Mmmm," she mumbled, downing her shake. Looking around the kitchen, she asked: "Lena gone already?" The housekeeper stayed overnights on weekends when Kat went to the cabin in Banff.

"Yeah, she had an early doctor's appointment."

Kat leaned over and kissed her son's cheek. He smiled up at her.

"Thanks for the good night-good morning, hello-good-bye kiss, Mom," he quipped.

"Have a great day at school," she retorted, not sure if it was a jab.

"And you have a great day at work," Sky said, standing to return her kiss.

"See you tonight." Kat threw on her coat, waved cheerily, grabbed her briefcase, and set off for the office to face the budget situation.

TWO

THE MINUTE KAT entered her chic modern office in downtown Toronto she was bombarded with questions. It was only 8 a.m., but the office was already in a flurry of activity, phones ringing, voices mingling, clerks fetching files, keyboards clicking, and the nearby coffee shop delivery being distributed. Kat handed off papers and files to various employees, shot brisk replies to their questions, and told those with materials for her to review to put them into her in-basket or send an email. Her personal secretary Sara came alongside with an iPad open to the day's agenda, making comments on the morning schedule. Kat gestured with a head nod that Sara should come into the large, minimalist yet elegant president's office with her.

"Everything set for the new store launch budget meeting?" Kat asked.

"Yes, the team's ready and will be here at 9 a.m sharp," Sara answered.

"And the investors' meeting?"

"We moved it to later in the day, since one key investor couldn't come at 2 p.m. Now set for 4 p.m., and everyone's OK with the change," Sara replied, checking the iPad schedule.

"That's better, gives me more time to digest the budget reports and fine-tune my presentation," Kat said.

Sara breathed an internal sigh of relief. She was really worried about Kat's reaction to the time change. Kat hated unexpected changes and often blew up at whoever brought the news.

"Anything else you need now, boss?" Sara asked.

"Make sure I've got the latest updated business plan file ready to go on my computer," Kat said. "Oh, and bring me a triple shot grande caramel mocha five minutes before the 9 a.m meeting." She wanted the caffeine and sugar to kick her brain into high gear.

"Check that." Sara turned and left the office on her errand.

Kat became engrossed in reviewing the business plan for the new Montreal store, and the hour flew past. Before she realized it, her staff was gathering in the conference room next to her office. Glancing through the one-way view glass wall in between the two rooms, she noticed them taking seats at the long oval table. She glanced at the wall clock, noting it was three minutes to 9 a.m. Where was that damn mocha? Just as she stood up to leave her office, Kat heard the door open, and Sara hurried in with the coffee. As their eyes met momentarily, Kat said nothing, but the daggers in her eyes stabbed Sara worse than any words could. Sara lowered her eyes, mumbled an apology, and quickly set the mocha down on Kat's desk, turning and scurrying out with shoulders hunched as if to ward off blows.

Taking a few sips of the decadently delicious caramel mocha, Kat felt a small wave of remorse. Sara was clearly terrified, and the killer look she had received from Kat was probably over the top. After all, the coffee was in her hands, and she had time for several sips before joining the meeting. *Just keep calm*, Kat thought to herself, remembering that self-talk was one of her father's many principles for life.

During the budget meeting, Kat learned that the marketing budget she had set was running low. Despite what she thought was sound financial advice from her experts, the costs of building and marketing the Montreal store were exceeding estimates. Not just a little, but going *way* over budget. As Kat listened to the details of why every aspect of construction was going to cost more than expected, along with city permits, safety inspections, mitigation fees, and so on, her mind was spinning. To top it all off, the marketing projections were escalating badly above anticipated costs.

Should she forget the whole thing? No, she wasn't a quitter; once she committed to something, she felt compelled to see it through. Should she scale back the store? That might not even be possible, given the contracts she had signed. Opening a diminished store in Montreal sounded like a failure already. If she cut back on the marketing plan, she was making failure more likely. She wasn't a loser; failure of her new store simply was not an option. What about getting more funds to meet the inflated budget? That seemed the best approach, but where would she get them?

Kat ran the borrowing possibilities through her mental checklist and quickly realized the investors would not give her additional loans for this store. Her budget team concluded that another $2.5 million would be needed to finish construction and carry out the marketing campaign. The only real solution she saw was to leverage another store. She called the head of store operations into the meeting, asked which of the 16 stores was most profitable and had the lowest amount of debt, and decided against issuing more stock to raise capital. The store would be leveraged by borrowing against it, and those funds used to complete and launch the new Montreal store. Her chief financial officer noted that the successful store would then be highly leveraged, with more debt than equity.

Kat gave the go-ahead to leverage the store. There was no way she could lose.

The 4 p.m business meeting with the new store investors went very well. Kat used the extra time given by the schedule change to tailor her presentation. She rephrased the financial data to make it appear everything was perfectly in place. By shifting most of the budget overrides to the marketing budget, she made the solid funding appear to satisfy construction costs and glossed over sources of additional funding for marketing. Her glib speech and distracting stories allowed her to slip past details of the leveraging.

She knew it was a lie and showed lack of integrity but had to do it. Kat couldn't stand not being in control and felt compelled to give the appearance of the exact opposite. On the inside, she was angry with herself. But winning, being successful, was worth everything. She had to be on top, and she couldn't stand the thought of being rejected.

After the meeting, several investors wanted Kat to join them for dinner and celebratory drinks. Kat was on edge because of her lies and shaky sense of control, but if she didn't go, they might think something was wrong. To subdue her anxiety, Kat had too many drinks with dinner and got a little sloppy, getting overly familiar and telling some lewd stories. Still, she never hinted at her financial woes. The investors, mostly men, were entertained by Kat's lively performance. Some took advantage of her inebriation to hug goodbye a bit too tightly. Normally she would deck a guy for that, except she was tipsy, and these were her investors.

It was nearly midnight when Kat steered her Mercedes Benz E 550 AMG Luxury Sedan a bit unsteadily into the condo's circular driveway. The valet, Felipe, opened her door and offered a hand, which she pushed aside. As she stepped out, he asked how her evening had gone.

"None of your damn business," Kat spat at him. "Just park the car."

"Yes, ma'am," Felipe said politely.

She was still stewing over the valet's presumptuousness as she let herself into the condo. Throwing her coat aside and kicking off her shoes, she wove toward the kitchen for a drink of water. On the table, she saw one place set for dinner, complete with wine glass and nice silver. A leftover pizza was covered with wrap beside the range. With a sinking feeling, she remembered that Sky said he would make her favorite pizza for dinner, and she'd promised to be there. Cursing to herself about forgetting dinner after being gone for a long four-day weekend, Kat gulped down two glasses of water, put the pizza in the fridge, and collapsed in bed.

THREE

SHRILL SPORTS WHISTLES repeated insistently, jarring Kat awake at 4 a.m. It took her groggy mind a few seconds to realize it was her alarm. Groaning, she slapped the snooze button and rested her pounding head back on the pillow. Time for the morning workout, the last thing in the world she wanted to do. For a nanosecond, she considered sleeping in, but her mental chorus kept shouting, "Relentless! No exceptions! Make the sacrifice to reach your goals! Get up and get going!"

Kat rolled out of bed, threw on some sweats, drank several glasses of water and called the limo to take her to the gym. Her head felt like it might explode and her stomach was queasy, but she gritted her teeth and with grim determination powered through a killer workout. She kept repeating, "You're gaining an edge, you're gaining an edge; fight the enemy, fight the enemy."

One of her father, Vince's, principles was called Fighting the Enemy. He said the Enemy was always laying in wait to divert you from your goals. The Enemy could be the opinions of others, poor habits, laziness, self-doubt, making excuses, and countless other things that could sabotage your efforts. "Nothing is neutral," Vince had said. "All your habits, routines, the actions you take or don't take, will compound over time either bolstering or detracting from your goals. Every decision you make either brings you closer or farther away. In each moment, make the intelligent decision, not the stupid one," he admonished.

Sticking to her routine was the intelligent decision, Kat knew. She wouldn't allow being hungover to become an excuse, relentlessly pushing herself through the grueling workout. After taking a shower and washing off the sweat, she actually felt better. *Nothing like over-exertion to work off a hangover*, she thought.

Back at home, she woke Sky up with a kiss and gently tousled his hair, reminding him it was time to get ready for school. During breakfast, she apologized for missing dinner the previous night, explaining her important night with investors but making it a point to say how sorry she was for forgetting. Sky smiled, knowing full well this was not the first time, nor would it be the last, that she completely forgot dinner he made for them.

"That's OK, Mom," Sky told her. "I'm really happy to have you back after the long weekend. I know your work can be very demanding. We'll have more dinners to share."

Sky's kindness and understanding began to penetrate her hard shell, and she fought back the stinging tears of remorse. Unable to speak without her voice quivering, she merely nodded. He insisted on cooking eggs for them both, telling her some solid protein would help restore her energy for the day ahead. She gratefully accepted, and they had a nice breakfast chatting about the day.

"I've got extra long baseball practice this week," Sky said. "We're getting ready for an important game against our main rivals in the league."

"How's your practice going?" Kat asked.

"Really well. I'm getting close to nailing my slider pitch, and that'll give us an edge Everyone on the team is playing at higher levels than a couple of months ago. We have a good chance to win."

"Wow! That's great!" Kat exclaimed, truly delighted at her son's abilities. "You need to keep your sights on playing MLB. I'm sure it's a goal you can accomplish if you set your target and work hard."

"Thanks, Mom. Just doing my best."

As they finished breakfast, the main entrance doorbell buzzer sounded, and the digital kitchen ID read out "Sky's chauffeur." Sky gathered his school pack, and they kissed goodbye. Trying to keep a level head and shift gears, Kat got ready for work and buzzed the valet to bring around her Mercedes.

Her mind was already on the day ahead at work when she walked out the main entrance to her waiting car. She felt uneasy with the lies she used to manipulate figures during the investors' meeting, worried about the consequences of over-levering a store and a bit disgusted at her sloppy behavior during dinner. The valet caught her off guard with his question as he opened the car door for her.

"How is your son Sky doing? He's been getting home later than usual recently."

Kat whipped her head around, doing a double-take at the valet. What kind of nerve did he have asking personal questions about her son? It was none of his business. She recalled telling him that several times, but he seemed never to get the message. And worse yet, making observations about their lives! This guy just did not know his place, and she was going to remind him of it.

"F**k off!" She yelled in his face. "Keep your lousy thoughts to yourself! Stay out of my family's business. I don't want to have to tell you again, or your job will be on the line."

Felipe's wounded expression was wholly lost on Kat as she whipped her head forward, slammed the car door and jammed the accelerator, leaving with a screech of tires.

The entire drive to the office, her mind was ranting about the audacious behavior of the valet, whose name she couldn't even remember. People in his position had no business probing into the life of condo residents. One more offense, and she was going to make a stink about it to condo management. Something just did not feel right about this situation.

Her mental rant soon transitioned to her work problems, how she would make certain the big leveraging against her most successful store would work out, how to minimize risk. She knew that leverage using borrowed capital had the potential to multiply returns from the project, but it also multiplied the risk of loss if the investment did not pan out. She had to take whatever steps were needed to avoid that risk. She'd better call another meeting with the marketing team, put some fire under their rears, and hammer on the critical importance of a successful store launch. All the while, she tried to ignore the uneasy feeling she was having about the entire project.

FOUR

KAT AWOKE AT 4 a.m again and set off for her 4:30 a.m workout, feeling a lot better than yesterday. Usually, the physically demanding gym machines, weights, ropes and spinners kept her mind from swirling with thoughts, but today not so much. The exchange she'd had with the condo valet still irked her, but she couldn't put her finger on why. His interest in her and Sky just seemed weird. She couldn't figure it out, so she pushed herself to work out harder and managed to shove the thoughts from her mind for the time being.

Back home after the gym, she begged off having breakfast with Sky using the "work emergency excuse" he had become accustomed to. It was clear that she was distracted, most likely due to work issues, so he told her that he understood, not to worry. She downed an antioxidant power shake and left for work.

First thing that morning, she had called a meeting with the store launch marketing team, and they were gathered in the conference room when she arrived. The team had prepared new estimates on how successful this store launch in Montreal would be, based on early Toronto store post-launch sales, with the added boost of novelty since this was her first store in a different city. Kat watched the numbers scroll across the large TV screen connected to the marketing team computer. Items were arranged by product category and timeline post-launch over six months, then over two years. The numbers looked quite good, but not good enough for Kat.

"What are your best top-range numbers for all product sales by six months?" she queried.

"Those could be an additional 10 percent," the lead marketing team member said. "Here, I'll bring up the slide showing bottom, middle, and top ranges by sales volume and dollar values."

He tapped the computer keyboard, and another set of figures and graphs appeared on the TV screen. Kat studied them carefully, running estimates against the repayment schedule for the leveraged $2.5 million. It was falling short of what would be needed. Her gut wrenched, but immediately she called up a new resolve. This store had to succeed, as failure was not an option. It had to reach even beyond the predictions the marketing team was showing.

"OK, so the additional 10 percent brings the numbers into an acceptable range," she said. "But I still want more. Get back to work on enhancing the marketing strategies to create increased sales volume both on the six-month and the two-year projections. We've got an augmented marketing budget now—take advantage of that and use your creative abilities. But stick to the new budget, no more overruns."

"Will do, boss," the team leader replied. "It would sure help to get a really big-name endorsement. We've got a few good ones, but a top-level influencer would be great."

"Check. I'll look into that right away," Kat said.

Kat fully understood the way that a famous influencer's endorsement would skyrocket sales. She had studied the impact of such influencers on both United States and Canadian businesses. It made the difference between hundreds of thousands and multiple millions in sales annually. These influencers had a vast online presence, including hundreds of millions of followers on Twitter and Instagram. They were newsworthy and appeared in regular media outlets, both virtual and print. The most famous had appeared in films and TV ads, some having a TV show or series of their own.

At the moment, Kat could not bring to mind a top-level influencer who she could court. She would devote some time to doing a web search later, after returning several pressing phone calls and dealing with daily chores of running a multi-store business.

In the mid-afternoon, Sara buzzed Kat's office line with "urgent" flashing on the phone's digital message. Kat picked up at once, curious what was up now.

"Boss, you've got a call from Cayla Cateau," Sara said breathlessly.

Kat was stunned. Cayla Cateau was exactly the type of top-level influencer she had been trying to bring to mind. Cayla was a big athletic influencer, a gold medal winner in the Winter Olympics the previous year, a TV personality and a social media phenomenon. In addition, Cayla was politically active, lobbying for good causes such as First Nation rights, women's opportunities in sports and limiting oil and gas extraction through fracking. Why hadn't she thought of Cayla? Heart pounding, Kat took the celebrity's call.

"Hello, Ms. Von Slyke," said the easily recognized voice of the athletic star. "It's Cayla Cateau, and I'm interested in doing an ad for TV featuring your line of sports clothes. I've used your brand and find the clothes and gear excellent, high quality, comfortable and stylish. Is this something you'd be interested in pursuing?"

Hell yes! thought Kat. Holding the phone, she tried to sound calm.

"I would most certainly be interested in an endorsement by you, Ms. Cateau," Kat replied in her most unruffled voice. "I'm a great fan of yours and follow your career closely. It's an honor to have your support for my products, and I can't thank you enough for your interest."

"Don't thank me; thank your charming employee Nancy Trevor. She's one of the most delightful marketing reps I've ever met. I can't stress how much fun we've had in our meetings and activities together. Nancy reached out to my team and had such convincing reasons why we should do this sponsorship that I simply had to meet her. So, we met for lunch, and we went ice skating a few times; she's a top-notch skater, almost kept up with me. I told her she should consider speed-skating tryouts for the next Olympics."

"Wow! I'm so glad you and Nancy had such a great connection. And I'm eager to get going on planning the TV ad for your endorsement as soon as possible. You probably know I've got a new store opening in Montreal in a few weeks. Your endorsement couldn't have come at a better time. It will make a huge difference to the new store's success."

The rest of the conversation dealt with details of their marketing teams working together and scheduling meetings for developing and producing the TV advertisement.

Kat was ecstatic. She never expected a "bluebird" to drop so fortunately into her hands. Immediately she called the head of marketing to inform him of the spectacular news and get him to work on the endorsement ad. Sara, of course, was eager to learn the upshot of the conversation with the athletic influencer, and soon word had spread throughout the office. As the day ended, Kat left the office full of confidence with a springy step. However, she had not mentioned Nancy's role in the coup; in the excitement, it must have slipped her mind. She gave a general high-five to everyone as she went out the door right past Nancy's desk, never noticing the young woman's expectant look turn into disappointment.

FIVE

THE ROUTINE CONTINUED with Kat waking at 4 a.m., doing her 4:30 a.m . workout, having breakfast with Sky, intense work all day, dinner meetings most nights, back home to check on her son's day before bedtime, sleeping. With dogged regularity, the drill repeated each day through the week until Friday arrived. Kat was looking forward to a weekend with her son, when she could have no more than the usual demands of work catch-up.

Every Friday, she held a weekly wrap-up meeting with heads of the various departments and projects. Each reported on the week's accomplishments and any problems encountered. She was given a written summary by in-house email with a deadline of 9 a.m. Friday. This gave her most of the day to read and make notes for the department heads' meeting that took place at 4 p.m. All 22 of the department heads were seated around the conference table when Kat walked in, notes ready on her iPad.

Her primary focus was on problems that could readily be fixed. Efficiency was upmost in her mind; she couldn't afford to waste time and effort on difficulties that involved complexities. Those she put on indefinite hold or closed down the project. Her business was suspended on a thin economic wire, one that might snap suddenly. Kat's perceived lack of control created the fear underlying her anger, competitiveness and insensitivity to others. Uncertainties about her business fed into this sense of being out of control, further driving her reactivity. Whatever she could control, she would control. If she lost control, she would frequently blow up.

When it came time for the manager of Store #5 to report, Kat listened for a few minutes, checked her iPad notes, and began interrogating him.

"Your report shows sales down 24% this week. Why is that?"

"I haven't clearly identified the reason yet," the worried manager responded.

"That's your job!" Kat looked the middle-aged man in the eye. "Need I remind you that a store manager's number one concern is how well their store is performing economically? The cost versus expenses bottom line? We're in a business here. We need efficient management, and that means staying on top of the reasons your store is doing well or not doing well. Give me your best guesses at why your sales are down."

The manager under attack swallowed hard, his eyes sliding away from Kat's piercing stare. His job was on the line, and he knew it. Kat had no tolerance for uncertainty and inefficiency.

"Uh . . . well, a competing sporting goods store just opened last week, just three blocks from ours. They ran lots of opening bargains, prices well below ours for those items. We did publicize our own bargains mid-week, hoping to counteract the impact on our sales. I thought this would compensate for the competition."

"Obviously it didn't. Probably too little too late. Anything else?"

"We ran out of stock on an especially popular style of tennis shoes," the manager said, clearly embarrassed and uncomfortable.

"Great! I'll bet the new competitor had plenty of those items in stock," Kat said with disgust dripping from her voice. "Fix this situation. Fix it now. And don't let something so stupid happen again. I want to see record sales from your store next week."

The store manager slumped down in his chair, mumbling that he would take care of things. Kat found a few other items in subsequent reports that could be fixed quickly, shot orders about how to accomplish them, and adjourned the meeting at 5 p.m. In her office afterward, checking a few messages and emails, she saw a call coming through on her private cellphone from her father, Vince. It surprised her since he rarely called her at work.

"Hi, Dad, what's up?" she said, answering the call.

"Hi, Kit-Kat." Her father was the only person who could call her that and get away with it. "I really want to see you this weekend; just you. How about arranging to come over?"

"I'll try, Dad, but it might be tough to come alone since I have Sky this weekend. We have some plans, and I've got a keynote speech to work on, too."

"I've already talked to Bryce, asked him to take Sky for the weekend and he said yes," Vince replied.

This information put Kat into a full halt. Why on earth had Vince made those arrangements with Bryce? Anger surged quickly about her father stepping on her plans like that. But the anger was immediately followed by a jolt of fear. He must have a terribly important thing to discuss, for him to make these plans in order to visit with her alone. Her need for control quickly gave way, and she felt quaky inside.

"Is something wrong? Are you all right?"

"I can't talk about things over the phone. I really do need you to come this weekend."

"Dad, please . . ."

"Just come over, kitten. It's important to me."

"All right, Dad." She was resigned that he would not reveal anything now. "I'll drive right over on Saturday after Bryce picks up Sky."

On the drive home, Kat felt her emotions taut and on edge. She tried to focus on keeping her cool, but the inner turmoil would not be quieted. She was deeply worried—actually nearly terrified—about what was happening with her father. Vince was such a strong anchor in her life that any uncertainties about his well-being seriously undermined her very foundation. She couldn't bear the suspense of waiting until the next day to learn what was up, so she decided to shift her focus back to work to keep her mind occupied.

When she thought about the department heads' meeting and how she skewered the manager of Store #5 in front of his peers, she felt bad. Of course he should have done a better analysis, but berating a team member in public went against good leadership principles. She should have called him in for a private conference. Inside, she was not happy with who she was becoming, how a flare of emotions made her treat people. She realized what was going on inside her was the source of her explosions, and that she needed to work on herself. This was something her father called the Inside-Out Process, and there were tools he had taught her for analyzing what was going on. But she didn't have time now for doing that work, and she just could not stop herself from reacting. With a deep sigh, she blamed her short fuse on the stress of the new store launch and her over-leveraged financial situation.

She pulled the Mercedes into the condo's circular driveway. Felipe, the valet, greeted her as he opened the door for her to get out.

"Good afternoon, Ms. Von Slyke," said Felipe. "I hope your work week went well. Good that it's Friday, huh? Do you and your son have weekend plans?"

Kat's anger erupted anew. There the nervy jerk was once more nosing into her life after she had warned against ever doing it again. She clamped her jaw against the reflexive insults she was about to discharge. He would get his come-uppance soon enough. Without so much as a glance in the valet's direction, she threw her keys onto the car seat and stormed through the entrance, fuming all the way up to her condo.

SIX

EVEN ON SATURDAY, Kat got up early and did her gym routine. She was still out of sorts, a mixture of worry and anger. Although she pushed the workout hard, her mind would not quiet down. She did not like herself this way but was unable to make things change. At breakfast with Sky, she told him that his father was coming soon to pick him up for the weekend. Sky was confused since this was his mom's scheduled weekend. Kat told Sky that something had come up: an unexpected and important meeting that she could not put off. At the moment, she didn't want to share her concerns about her father. The situation was too unclear, too uncertain.

Sky looked disappointed but did not push for more explanations. He sensed that his mom was on edge, clearly disturbed by something. She had been under a lot of stress lately around the launch of the new store, and he assumed this was another problem related to that. He was actually a little relieved to spend the weekend with his father, whose life seemed happier and more balanced than his mom's life.

Since the divorce three years ago, Bryce had remarried and now had a 2-year-old daughter named Grace. Sky liked his stepmother, who was a kind and loving person, always reaching out and interested in his activities. His baby half-sister was really cute, too, and she babbled and bounced in delight during their games. It wouldn't be so bad to spend the weekend with them.

Bryce came up to the condo after Kat buzzed him in. Sky let him inside with a big hug, remarking that he would get his overnight bag and be right back.

"How are things, Kat?" Bryce asked cheerfully.

"All right," she lied. "Things going well with you?"

"Just fine. I was more than happy to take Sky when Vince called me. We don't have any plans this weekend, just hanging at home. Evelyn says Sky is always welcome, not to hesitate."

Kat flinched at the mention of Bryce's wife, Evelyn. She made an effort to be polite.

"That's nice, please thank her for me," Kat said, struggling to stay even-tempered.

"Is Vince OK? He sounded tired when he called," Bryce said.

"I don't know; he wouldn't give me details. Do me a favor, don't tell Sky that Vince requested the weekend exchange. I don't want Sky to worry. I told him it was due to my work."

Bryce looked quizzically at Kat but nodded his agreement.

Sky returned with his bag, hugged Kat and left with his dad. Kat struggled with mixed emotions, glad that Bryce and Sky had a close relationship, but jealous of the warm family environment her ex-husband had created after leaving her.

Driving the 50-minute trip to her father's house, Kat wondered why he told her to come there, and not to his favorite restaurant where they usually met for lunch. It was called The Stadium, aptly named sitting right next to the Toronto Blue Jays baseball stadium. Vince had had a successful career playing professional baseball with the Blue Jays as a star pitcher, then became a coach for some years and now worked as general manager of the team. It was important for him to stay connected with the team and contribute to their continuing success. The fact that her father was deviating from the usual routine today only added to Kat's worries.

After arriving at Vince's house and exchanging greetings, Kat and Vince sat at the dining table, which was set for a cold-cut sandwich lunch. Kat still felt the emptiness of the house without her mother, who had died five years ago. She often thought about how Vince managed to stay positive and seemed content with life after losing his wife. He'd always had the ability to stay focused and see beyond his circumstances, even the most trying ones. It was a trait she really admired.

"Well, Dad, what's so important that I had to upend my weekend plans and come for a visit?" Kat had intended to stay calm, but irritation spilled out. "You know, I'm working on a keynote speech for the Young Professionals Association conference in two weeks. This is really cutting into my time this weekend to work on it."

"No, I didn't know that," Vince said. "You can spend time working on your speech tomorrow. I realize it's important to you, Kat. Your business really seems to drive your life. I'm proud of what you've accomplished, but there's more to life than a successful career. Did you ever consider that you might have your priorities misplaced?"

Kat was taken aback by her dad's comment. Success had seemed important in his career, and he pushed hard when playing baseball and coaching.

"How are my priorities misplaced? I thought you put a high value on success."

"I've often emphasized that there are other important things in addition to success. These things are necessary to bring real joy and happiness; to live a *truly* successful life. Like our relationships, family, friends, people we love and cherish. The places, experiences and things we share with each other, like health, personal growth and spirituality. You remember, it's my model of the 8 Forms of Wealth, or the Wheel of Life. I've been thinking a lot about our life cycles, what true wealth and success are, as of late."

Vince fell silent, gazing off into the distance. Red flags were going up in Kat's mind; she knew something was seriously wrong. Why was her dad focusing on the Wheel of Life? For the first time, she noticed how worn-down her father looked. He had lost weight and had an ashen tint to his skin. Her heart was pounding.

"Dad, for God's sake, tell me what's going on!" Her voice was quavering with fear.

"OK. I don't know any gentle way to say this, so here it is. I've been diagnosed with an aggressive form of prostate cancer. It snuck up on me, no symptoms for years, and then suddenly, I felt fatigued, short of breath, and weak. Not like myself at all. Went to the doctors, had the tests, and got the verdict. Widespread aggressive cancer, now in my lungs and bones. Doesn't look good." He dropped his head into his hands.

"Oh my God, Dad, no!" Kat felt wild as the roaring emotions flooded her body. "Not cancer. Not that. Are the doctors sure? Can you get second opinions?"

"Believe me; I did have several consultants. They all agreed on the diagnosis. They plan to start with radiation to shrink the largest tumors, followed by several rounds of chemotherapy. At best, these treatments can retard the cancer; keep it at bay for some time. The specialists don't offer much hope of a cure. But I can always hope, and I do. I'm a fighter, you know that. I'll fight this cancer. The treatments will put me under a bit, make me sick and weak for a while. We start treatment on Monday."

Vince looked into his daughter's eyes, which were wide with disbelief. Her face registered shock and despair.

"Keep close to me, Kat. I'll need to draw on your strength for a time."

SEVEN

PAINFUL MEMORIES SURGED unbidden into Kat's mind. She saw her younger brother Max's face clearly, as scenes from his illness and death flashed in vivid mental images. He had died from cancer at 11 years old, when Kat was 15. It was leukemia, and Max faced it with the courage of a champion. He went through a course of radiation and chemotherapy, lost his hair, went into remission, had a recurrence and another round of treatments, and went into remission again. Throughout his battle, he continued to engage in life, especially his love of sports. He never complained and kept positive. Then, just when it seemed he was finally cured, two years into his second remission, the leukemia returned. His young body could not withstand another round of radiation and chemotherapy. His only chance was bone marrow transplant, and Kat was the best-matched donor.

Kat readily agreed and went through the grueling and painful procedure of extracting her bone marrow with long needles. Even so, she felt that her suffering was much less than Max's, and she was glad to do anything to help. At first, Max did great—he seemed his former energetic self, and the family rejoiced as his discharge day approached. But, it didn't last: His body rejected the bone marrow transplant. Soon his organs were shutting down, he went into a coma and died two days later.

When the devastated family went home, now without Max, Kat felt a weight pressing on her heart that she could not lift. The agony of seeing her mother crumbling to her knees wracked by violent sobbing was burned indelibly into Kat's memory. Her body went numb but somehow still seared with pain as the horror dawned that her marrow may have been what killed her brother. Both her parents and the doctors assured her it was not her fault; these rejections were always a risk, no matter *who* gave the marrow.

Still, grief and anger flooded through her. She felt broken, despairing, empty. It was her dad who pulled the family through this tragedy. He took leave from his baseball career and stayed home to be a support every day. He reminded them that Max would always be with them; that they would never forget, and could get through this by sticking together.

Lost in the painful memories, Kat didn't notice when her dad moved and took a seat in the chair beside her. The weight of his still-strong arm around her shoulders brought her back into the present. She felt numb, at a loss for words, struggling to hold it together. She did not want to be weak. Her dad needed support, so she had to be strong. Reflexively, she took hold of his hand.

"The first round of therapy starts Monday, as I said. It should be finished in ten weeks. Then there's a break to let my body recover and gain strength. That gets us through the summer, and another round starts in early fall. We'll know how effective treatment is after that's completed." Vince kept his voice low and steady, but when Kat glanced at him, she saw tears collecting in his eyes.

Visions of her surgical prep before the bone marrow extraction coalesced. The cold, metal operating table, stark white walls, huge blinding light overhead, doctors and nurses with masks and caps on so only their eyes were visible. She was frightened and alone. She knew it would be painful. She struggled mightily to be brave, have courage for her brother Max.

Vince's hand wiped tears from her cheeks that she did not know were there. Slowly, the tears kept trickling, unbidden as she felt the sorrow and helplessness and loss piercing her heart. In a tangle of emotions, her grief mingled with anger and guilt. Vince hugged her tightly as they huddled in silence, sharing their sadness through tears.

At length, Kat sat upright, used a napkin to wipe her tears, and looked into her father's eyes. Though his eyelashes were still damp, he was gathering his emotions together, just as she was.

"OK, Dad. Wow, it's terrible . . . I'm so sorry . . . Please go through the diagnosis and treatment plans again. I want to understand. The shock of hearing that you're facing cancer threw me back into painful memories . . . you know . . ." Her voice trailed off.

Vince nodded. He fully understood that she was reliving her brother's struggle with cancer and his soul-wrenching death. Taking a deep breath, Vince repeated everything he had told Kat shortly before. She focused and paid close attention, asking questions for clarification. She told him that she would come to the cancer treatment center with him for the onset of therapy. He tried to reassure her that was not necessary, but she insisted. It would only be a day away from the office. She let him know how much she really wanted to be there.

In her mind, she realized she wanted to be present and supportive for him, just like he had been for her when Max died.

They eventually tried to eat the lunch Vince had prepared, but neither had any appetite. Father and daughter stretched out the nibbling just to spend time together. They talked of other insignificant things, such as the weather and local news. Time was needed for their raw emotions to settle down, for some semblance of normalcy to return in their lives. By late afternoon, Vince said he felt exhausted and wanted to take a nap. Kat was also strung out emotionally and ready to leave. They hugged, said goodbye, and promised to talk daily.

On the drive home, Kat felt both physically and emotionally drained. She rolled over in her mind just how to tell Sky about his grandfather's serious cancer. No good ideas surfaced, so she agreed with herself to deal with this later. When flashes of memory about Max threatened to deluge her, or images surfaced of her encounter with her dad that day, she stuffed them down fiercely. These were simply too painful. She hated feeling so unable to control things. She needed some kind of relief.

She keyed the car phone Bluetooth on voice command. Quickly she ran through a mental list of her friends who liked to drink and get rowdy. Picking four names, she called them in succession with the same message.

"Hey, guys, having a hard time. Need some drinks and laughs tonight. Meet me around 8 p.m. at Scotty's Pub."

EIGHT

ROCK MUSIC POUNDED Kat's ears as the band yowled unintelligible lyrics, and electric guitars wailed. Sweaty bodies twisted and gyrated, pressed together on the small dance floor. Body odor blended with the scent of cheap rum and tequila as dancers collided, laughing and bouncing off each other. The clock struck midnight just as the band ended a number. Kat did not care. She let her mind drift, thoughts fuzzy far in the background. As the next set began, Kat threw back her head and whooped, leaping into wild action and bouncing off sweaty men and drunken women who danced with equal abandon.

Had she stopped to think about it, Kat would admit that she fit right in with the crowd. Just a girl looking for some release, having a good time and forgetting her troubles. But her alcohol-dazed mind did not have any coherent thoughts. That was exactly what she wanted.

After the set ended, Kat's group of girlfriends were tired of dancing and returned to their VIP table next to the window. She felt ready to sit with them. Vaguely she heard their pointless conversation, tried to pay attention, but soon drifted into her own thoughts. That was a mistake, she realized. As soon as her body settled down, her mind returned to images of her dead brother and her father's haggard face at lunch. She couldn't bear those images and the sharp stabs of pain they brought. Summoning the waiter, she ordered more drinks for the table. Taking several gulps of her rum and coke, she tried to focus again on the conversation. Things were getting fuzzier.

Next thing she knew, she was on the dance floor once again. A blur of thrashing arms and twisting bodies filled her vision; her mind again blank as pounding music took it over. Time passed; she was dimly aware of returning to their table, going to the restroom, having more drinks, dancing again, and repeating this sequence again and again. The night melded into a jumbled pattern. She had no idea what time it was, and frankly, she did not care.

A group of guys pulled up chairs and joined the girls at their VIP table. Everyone was equally drunk and found silly conversation hilarious. Kat started to sober up after the guys arrived, some semblance of an alert going off in her bleary brain. She did not drink on the next round, asking instead for water. One of the men shifted his chair closer to her and started a conversation, asking about her work. Loose-tongued from her load of alcohol, Kat began babbling about work, a topic she knew and loved, and the guy appeared transfixed. She got friendlier due to his interest, and started to talk about her current business problems, but caught herself quickly. Turning the subject to his work, she tried to listen but still felt out of focus. She drank more water, sensing the need to get sober.

The man got forward with Kat, rubbing her arm and pressing his thigh against hers. Before long, he was inviting Kat to come to his place where he would show her a really good time. She refused, but he tried again, flattering her and hinting at his prowess. At this point, Kat gave him a blank stare, shook off his arm, and moved her chair back from the table. She stood up and told her girlfriends it was time for her to leave.

Everyone at the table protested, guys and girls alike, saying the fun was just beginning. Kat shook her head and repeated in a firm voice that she had to go. Through their chorus of wails and moans and flippant goodbyes, she turned and walked out of Scotty's Bar. On the way to her car, Kat realized she was walking unsteadily and not sober enough to drive. She texted for an Uber, which arrived within minutes. Kat climbed in and gave directions home to the East Indian driver who spoke with a thick accent. The Uber driver tried to strike up a conversation, which annoyed Kat and caused her anger to flare. She wondered why these foreign lackeys were always so nosy and pushy. She told him to just turn on the radio to whatever station popped up.

It was a religious station with a mellow-voiced pastor in the middle of a sermon about anger. Against her will, Kat was drawn into listening.

"Anger is a beast that eats up the hearts of men. It will consume your mind and bend your will. It will destroy your friendships and hurt your family. It will change success to failure. As James 1:19 advises us, 'My dear brothers and sisters, take note of this: Everyone should be quick to listen, slow to speak and slow to become angry.'

'What do you gain by venting your anger? Will doing this get you to where you want to be? Listen and be guided by the Lord's wisdom in Proverbs 29:11: 'A fool always loses his temper, but a wise man holds it back.' A hasty temper is nothing but courting folly. Nothing is gained and much can be lost when your anger gets out of control. If you ask with a sincere heart, God will change you and help you get rid of your anger. It doesn't matter how awful your situation is, the Lord's power is greater than any earthly events. Just open your heart and invite God in, ask Him to take anger away from your mouth. You are God's beloved, my friend; you are holy in the Lord's eyes. Yes, you are loved by God, and you deserve better than to suffer from what your anger, your short temper, your intolerance, your resentment are doing to you.

'Take heed, my friend, to what the Bible says about being slow to anger. 'The anger of man does not achieve the righteousness of God,' James 1:20 says. Don't let your anger lead you to sin against God's righteousness. Follow the example given in Ephesians 4:26 and 'Do not let the sun go down on your anger.'"

Kat felt smitten by these words that seemed aimed directly at her. She noticed a surge of anger and wanted to reject these ideas. Immediately she was flooded with shame and guilt as she remembered how her dad had taught her to control her emotions and her mind. Letting anger get the best of you was giving your power away. Blindly reacting to people or situations meant losing your power to them. But she was losing herself in the trauma of her brother's and father's cancers. Guilt seared her when thinking of her brother, how her bone marrow donation probably killed him. And now her father had cancer that was likely going to kill him.

She felt broken, despairing, empty. Her rage receded, and profound sadness came to take its place.

The radio minister was talking about forgiveness and how that would disarm anger. He said not only to forgive others, but to turn inward. Ultimately, forgiving yourself was what God called for in ousting the beast of anger. It was more than Kat could take.

'Change the radio channel!' she yelled at the Uber driver.

'What do you want, miss?' he asked.

'Anything, whatever, just some music.'

Bouncy melodies of a Spanish music station filled the car, and Kat let her mind go into pause as the repetitious rhythms droned on.

NINE

SOMEONE WAS BLOWING a shrill sports whistle over and over again. Why was someone doing that? Was the game over? She didn't remember what game or where, what team she was playing for or against. Had she missed Sky's baseball game again? Kat struggled through sodden layers of brain fog, trying to grasp what was happening.

STOP! Her mind screamed. *Just stop, stop now!* But the whistle kept repeating, piercing into her alcohol-toxic mind that simply could not grasp the scenario. She tried to open her eyes, but the lids seemed heavier than lead. She realized her head was pounding in rhythm with the whistle, and it felt as if her brain would explode. The whistle kept a steady pace as it slowly dawned on Kat that her alarm was going off. She had left it set for 4 a.m. before collapsing into bed a couple of hours earlier. Cursing, she punched the alarm off and lay there, head spinning.

Unbidden thoughts crept through the haze of semi-awareness. Kat tried to remember how she had become so drunk. Vague images materialized of the crowded bar, throbbing music, voices laughing, bodies colliding, sweat dripping, and a guy trying to hit on her. How did she get home? Oh yeah, took an Uber. Well, at least she wasn't so wasted that she tried to drive. She left her car at the bar parking lot, about five miles away. It would be OK there until she could get it today.

Other thoughts began to surface as she drifted in and out of consciousness. The new store launch was about to happen, and she was more than a little worried. It had to be a smashing success. Especially since she had leveraged so much to fund it, which wasn't such a smart decision in hindsight. The visit with her father replayed in her mind. She had not wanted to go, became impatient, and then was slammed with the news of his illness. Cancer. It couldn't be worse, despite his attempt to be positive. Painful memories flashed of her brother's fight against and ultimate defeat by cancer. Again, she was flooded by remorse at the idea that her donated bone marrow led to his death. She felt helpless; unable to affect the illnesses, and unable to control her emotions.

A wave of nausea swept through Kat, and she rolled out of bed and staggered to the bathroom. Hanging onto the toilet seat, she hurled the contents of her stomach into the bowl in repeated retches that left her shaking and faint. Breaking into a cold sweat, she felt consciousness slipping away as she passed out on the tile floor. It was several hours later when she awoke, cold to the bone, stiff muscles aching. She pulled herself up to the sink and washed her face with cold water, shivering uncontrollably. Grabbing her robe and clutching it around her, Kat made an unsteady way into the kitchen. It was 8 a.m., and she needed coffee—badly. Head still pounding, she set the coffee to brew and returned to the bathroom for aspirin. Coffee and aspirin, that would help some. She had missed her morning workout but figured she wouldn't be able to stomach it anyway.

What did she have to do today? There was something important this morning, she knew. After two cups of coffee and four aspirins, the head-pounding relented enough for Kat to remember that Sky had a baseball game at 10 a.m. He had gone to stay with Bryce while she visited with her father. Bryce would bring him to the game. She just had enough time to dress and walk the five miles to get her car. Walking would help clear her head, and she needed the exercise.

The morning air was cool and crisp, soft sunlight filtering through wispy clouds high above. Kat wore sunglasses, and still, the brightness hurt her eyes. She set a quick pace, but not fast enough to jar her brain that was still aching. *Getting drunk was not the smartest idea*, she mused. Her actions irritated her; she hated the feeling of losing control. And, she seemed to be losing control in too many ways: drinking too much, not able to control her stomach, her brother's death, and now her father's cancer. She tried to shake the thoughts off and focus on walking. There wasn't much traffic, and the streets were quiet. She drew deep breaths of fresh air into her lungs in an attempt to clear her mind.

It worked for a little while, but the annoying thoughts soon resurfaced. She reflected once again on how out of control she was feeling lately. She just wasn't staying on top of things. Another litany of offenses marched through her mind: She missed dinner with Sky, was short-tempered with her father, snapped at the valet, drank too much with investors and friends, and got a bit sloppy. She criticized her best assistant and called one of the store managers on the carpet in front of his peers. It was bad leadership behavior, she knew.

Another wave of nausea surged upward, more emotional than physical. Kat was sick of how she'd been feeling and behaving lately. She was angry with herself for letting these things get out of control. But, she could not seem to stop these reactions and couldn't pinpoint why. What was this internal drive that just would not let her stop? The aching in her head increased just thinking about it.

Mercifully, Kat arrived at her car and her mind was distracted with checking that all was OK. There did not appear to be any attempt to break in, the tires were still full and un-slashed, the windows unbroken. Scotty's Pub was in a pretty good area of town, but still, vandalism did happen occasionally. Sliding into the driver's seat, Kat was relieved to see her briefcase where she had left it, stuck halfway under the passenger seat. She pulled it out and removed her tablet. There was still enough time for a little work before driving off to Sky's baseball game. Shoving her feelings aside, she turned the tablet on and began working on her keynote speech for the Young Professionals Organization.

TEN

KAT MOVED OVER to the passenger seat and placed her tablet on her lap. Fingers poised over the small keyboard, she thought about the focus of her keynote speech for the YPO. They wanted to know how she became successful, why her career had skyrocketed in just a few years. She reflected on her career and how well her sports clothing and accessories business had done. What factors, she pondered, had contributed most to this result? As ideas rolled around in her mind, three words kept coming up: drive, motivation, and relentlessness. Achieving the goal was everything, and she wouldn't let anything stand in her way.

Don't let anything stand in your way, she thought. Did that mean people—family, friends, her son? The thought troubled Kat because it was not what she was taught growing up. The importance of family, of connections with people, had always been something her parents emphasized. She had passed these same values along to Sky, trying to regularly make time to do things together, check in about school, and remain curious about his interests and experiences. Somewhere along the line, however, this almost fanatical devotion to high-octane success had been injected into her values. The discrepancy puzzled her. It seemed impossible for close family relations to coexist with relentless pursuit of success, particularly if you refused to let anything come before achieving the goal.

Now her head was hurting again, and she realized that thinking so hard about these contradictions in values was causing brain pain. Glancing at the time, she realized that she had to leave right away to get to Sky's game before it began. With a small sigh of relief, she quit thinking and started the car, now intent on finding the quickest route to Sky's game. She made good time, parked, and climbed into the bleachers to see Sky's team warming up on the field. Sky saw his mom taking a seat and waved cheerily. She gave a pleasant wave back, glad that she had arrived before the first inning began.

Bryce and his wife Evelyn were seated several rows above Kat, and she did not see them. Watching Sky's fluid motions as he wound up and threw pitches occupied her attention. When she became aware of a man approaching her, she felt startled at first but then recognized Bryce. He sat in an open space beside her, greeting Kat without touching her.

'Hi, Kat. Good to see you. Things doing OK with you?" Bryce said.

"Good enough," she replied brusquely. "And you?"

"Everything is fine with us. We enjoyed having Sky over this weekend. Evelyn just loves how he plays with little Grace. Sky is such a pleasure to be around."

Kat nodded and looked straight ahead, watching Sky intently. She really did not want a conversation with Bryce right now. He waited a few minutes, and then continued.

"I was curious about why Vince called me and asked us to take Sky for the weekend. Is everything all right with him? I hope he's not having a problem and needed your help, or something like that."

"Vince is . . . uh, it's not something he wants me to talk about," said Kat. "Not to worry; it's just something personal. Family stuff, you know."

"Uh-huh. Well, let me know if I can do anything," said Bryce, feeling the rebuff.

In the tense silence that followed, Kat felt both angry at the situation and wrong about needing to detour around the truth. She was definitely not ready to have that conversation with Bryce.

"Things going well with work? I seem to recall that you've got a new store launching in a few weeks," Bryce said, making small talk.

"Yeah, sure. Couldn't be better." Kat looked away from Bryce to catch sight of Sky waving, but not at her. Sky was looking at someone higher in the bleachers. Kat turned and looked up; several rows above were Evelyn and Grace. Both were enthusiastically waving back to Sky, who grinned widely.

This exchange set Kat's teeth on edge. Resentment flared at the happy little moment of domestic affection. It was amply clear that her son was very fond of his stepmother and half-sister. Something inside Kat was shutting down, falling into a black hole in a flurry of despair and anger. She was staring directly into Evelyn's eyes, and in that instant, realized her scathing look sent daggers straight at the other woman. Evelyn appeared startled, her smile disappeared, and her eyes widened. Kat quickly turned away, hoping that Bryce had not observed this interchange. But he had, and his sad expression revealed his feelings.

"Kat, what's the matter with you?" he asked softly. "You seem really unhappy and on edge all the time. You're working too hard, driving too much. You've achieved huge success, why not relax and enjoy it? All that business success, is it actually bringing you more happiness? It may bring financial security, but there's so much more to life. I admire your drive, your commitment, and I always respected that part of you when we were together. But, Kat, it started consuming you and has only progressed. It's taking away from other areas of your life. Have you ever reflected about it? You are so successful in nearly every area of life, but all you've attained doesn't seem to bring true happiness. I think you know that."

For a few minutes, Kat simply stared at Bryce. In that moment, Kat saw herself as Bryce was seeing her. It didn't look good. A flash of insight revealed that her priorities were all mixed up; that he was right. She couldn't take observing herself right at that moment and pushed the troubling thoughts away. Shaking her head slowly, she narrowed her eyes, grimacing with clenched teeth as she retorted.

"You've got no right to pass judgment on my life. You can't possibly know what I'm up against. You can take that 'holier than thou' attitude and stuff it you know where."

Bryce lifted his hands as if warding off her attack. He moved his body reflexively, sliding a short distance away on the bench.

"I'm not trying to pick a fight," he said. "We've done more than enough of that. I just want you to know that I'm truly concerned about you. Pardon my frankness, but today you look terrible. Kind of wasted, and really fatigued. It's clear you're under a great deal of stress."

Kat's shoulders sagged, and she sighed, turning her head away from Bryce.

"OK, I am stressed, I am tired, and I drank too much last night. But that's none of your concern. You're not involved in my life that way anymore. Keep your advice to yourself."

Bryce shrugged and stood up to leave.

"Whatever you want. Let's each return to our separate spheres and watch the game."

"Fine with me." Kat refused to look at Bryce as he slowly climbed the bleachers to join his wife and daughter.

ELEVEN

DURING THE FOLLOWING week, Kat finished writing her keynote speech for the YPO. She focused in on the motivational part, giving particular emphasis to the determination and relentless drive necessary to achieve big goals. There was no hint of her current difficulties and no mention of the human toll such one-pointed ambition demanded. In fact, Kat herself had hardly begun to acknowledge this. On Friday, she delivered the speech to a local group of Toastmasters. They were taking a video that she could watch later and use to make improvements as needed. It was perfect practice for the important conference a few weeks following.

Dressed smartly in sleek, professional style, Kat had a commanding presence as she delivered her speech flawlessly. The AV connections worked perfectly, and the audience seemed captivated. She ended with a power-packed summary:

"To achieve this kind of success, you've got to stay 'in the zone.' For me, this is a wholehearted pursuit toward a single, clear goal. All distractions are ignored in the zone. Every ounce of mental, physical, emotional, and intellectual strength and energy is 100% dedicated to the task at hand. Any distraction threatening your focus must be removed. Being in the zone leads to peak performance, which brings you as close to the human potential as possible. It brings you to the top of your game. Peak performers stay in the zone through all the seasons of their careers.

"Remember the tools for success that I've discussed. With these tools up your sleeve, get to work! The time is now. I'm really passionate about taking immediate action. My commitment to relentlessly pursuing success by taking immediate action opened more opportunities than I could have dreamed. It's time to start pursuing your goals and your dreams. It's time to start living world-class. It's time to become a peak performer. It's time to find relentless success!"

The Toastmasters group broke into a round of enthusiastic applause. Kat smiled, thanked them, and invited comments or questions. She fielded the first several questions easily, but was taken aback when the topic switched to the sacrifices required for relentless success.

"What about the personal side of life?" asked a serious-looking young woman. "It seems that the time and energy demanded by such single-minded focus will take away from relationships, such as your family and friends."

"We have to make sacrifices to achieve big successes and live world-class," Kat replied. "I'm not telling you to ignore relationships, but to keep them from interfering with goals. It's a balancing act."

"It sounds like there's not much time for just having fun, enjoying life," another woman said. Several people around her were nodding their heads.

"Yes," one added. "I feel the need for more humanity, balance—you know, the personal side of life. Our careers aren't everything."

Kat felt confused but did not let it show. She replied with some generalities about keeping career and personal life in balance, although she knew this was anything but true in her own situation. As the session ended, quite a few people offered praise and congratulations for both the speech and her accomplishments. This soothed her but did not remove the uncertainty clouding her mind. A small group had planned dinner with her afterward, and they set off for a nice restaurant nearby.

The restaurant was called Status, located in a tower building overlooking Toronto harbor, billed as "elegant fine-dining with city views and a menu of upscale Canadian fare." Everyone ordered a round of drinks first, and wine with dinner. Kat downed her Royal Crown Canadian Whiskey and soda quickly, had another, and drank liberally of the crisp, grassy Sauvignon Blanc that came with their meals. The group's jollity level soon surpassed fine dining standards, and the waiter politely asked the table to keep their voices down, as he had received a noise complaint from other diners. This worked for around 30 minutes, but as stories were swapped and alcohol freely consumed, their table drew another admonition against being too noisy.

Kat's dander was up after this second reproof. She made a point of continuing to talk loudly and gesticulate dramatically while expounding her theory of physical conditioning, including 4:30 a.m. gym workouts daily without exception. Swinging her arm widely, she knocked over her wine glass, its contents spilling across the tablecloth while everyone shrieked and dabbed with napkins. Kat was laughing hysterically when the waiter returned and stood beside her.

"Ma'am, I'd like you to accompany me to see the manager," he said firmly.

"Wha-aat?" she gasped, continuing to laugh. "Cool down; we're just having fun."

"Yes, ma'am, but you are disturbing other guests. Please come with me now."

"Don't make such a big deal out of things, loosen up. C'mon, man!"

The group around the table fell silent, staring at Kat, who was obviously tipsy, and back to the waiter who appeared flushed and embarrassed. His bulky frame hovered over Kat, round belly brushing the back of her chair.

"I really must insist that you come now to see the manager," the waiter repeated.

"Oh, go along with him, Kat," one man at the table said. "Humor them, let's not make a scene."

"Yeah, at least not more of a scene than we've already made," added a woman, giggling.

"Well, all right!" Kat exclaimed. "Anything to please my friends."

The waiter pulled back her chair as she rose and walked beside him. She was quiet at first, but just couldn't keep her mouth closed.

"If you're going to get what you want, you have to stop being a pathetic shadow of a man," Kat said, too loudly for decorum. "Don't pawn me off on the manager. Stand firm, be a man, and tell me what you want. While you're at it, hit the gym and take care of yourself, you pig."

Jowly face flushed nearly magenta, the chubby waiter hurried out of the dining room and down the hall toward the manager's office, Kat traipsing behind, laughing and repeating "such a pig, mere shadow of a man." Suddenly she realized that the manager, a tall and muscular man, was standing in the hall, glaring at her.

"She just won't stop talking loud and laughing, it's disturbing other customers," the waiter said. "And she insulted me."

"I heard it," said the manager. "It's OK; I'll take care of it." Nodding, the dejected waiter shuffled back down the hall.

"Ms. Von Slyke, I believe? This kind of behavior is not acceptable at Status. You will have to leave now." His voice was hard, and his expression firmly set.

"What do you mean? We're just friends having a good time. We come here often and spend lots of money. We're regular customers; we deserve special treatment," Kat complained.

"It doesn't matter how often you come or how much you spend," the manager retorted. "If you make a scene and other customers are offended, you're not welcome here."

"That's just plain stupid!" Kat yelled. "Why can't we enjoy ourselves?"

"You're inebriated and out of control. You have to leave now. I'll walk you to the door after you get your things at the table."

"Huuuh? You're throwing me out?"

"Yes, ma'am. Don't make me call the police."

TWELVE

THE FLIP OF a lightswitch jarred Sky awake. He covered his eyes with his hands and heard his mom's voice. "Time to get up and going. See you at breakfast in a few."

As his eyes adjusted, Sky tried to recall when his mom got home last night. It must have been really late because he had already gone to bed. She was doing that a lot more lately. It worried him, as she seemed to be troubled by something.

Sky rolled out of bed and immediately hit the floor. Still in pajamas, he did 20 pushups to start the morning exercise routine. He was committed to daily exercise, but not starting as early as his mom did. He admired his mom's enthusiasm but was simply unwilling to get up at 4 a.m. like a crazy person to work out. There were lots of opportunities during the day for what he needed to do to stay in shape.

After a few minutes of warming up with calisthenics, he walked to his bedroom door to look at the attached whiteboard. This was one way that he used the morning routine to affirm his goals. On the board was a label titled "Big Dream" and below it, he had written in large bold letters "Professional Pitcher." This provided an affirmation of his utmost goal. Seeing it written on his door every morning was a strong reinforcement and kept him focused. Under this was an "Action Plan," and the next entry was "Select Team Tryouts." The due date was one day away. He had been practicing every day, keeping his pitching arm in shape, pushing for greater precision and accuracy. He felt good about his progress and ready for the tryouts.

Stretching out his pitching arm, he grabbed a rolled-up pair of socks and threw them into the laundry basket with perfect aim. Just for reassurance, he sent a second pair sailing into the laundry basket in almost exactly the same trajectory. Nodding with satisfaction, Sky shook out his arm, got dressed and headed to the kitchen for breakfast.

Kat was cooking pancakes and dished up a short stack on Sky's plate. She had already had her morning power shake. Sky cut up some fruit and gave her a small bowl, which she was glad to have, and they sat at the table chatting.

"How was your practice speech at Toastmasters last evening?" Sky asked.

"Good. It went pretty well, just a few minor changes I'll probably make," Kat replied.

"Do you feel ready for the YPO conference?" he mumbled while chewing the pancakes covered with maple syrup, his favorite.

"Pretty much." Kat stared off into the distance as if preoccupied with a heavy thought.

Sky glanced at her face as she looked off. She appeared haggard, with dark circles under her eyes. She must not have gotten much sleep last night, probably came in really late, and drank too much at dinner. He was concerned that this was becoming a pattern.

Changing the topic, Kat asked about his tryouts the next day and if he felt ready. He assured her of his confidence and optimism that he would do well. But, she appeared inattentive, only half listening to what he was saying. He wondered if the new store launch was causing the distraction.

"Everything going as planned for the Montreal store launch?" he asked.

"Uh . . . yeah, sure, things are going along according to schedule," Kat replied. Something in her tone alerted him that this might not be entirely true.

"Any unexpected glitches? It's such a big event, lots of moving parts, wouldn't be surprising if something was not quite right."

"Oh, there's nothing out of the ordinary. Just the usual complexities, you know, lots of parts flying around. It'll all be fine." Kat was not looking at Sky as she said this. He knew something was up, but could not put his finger on it. There were things she was not saying, and her vague answers troubled him. Usually, she was more candid with him about her business and seemed to appreciate being able to share about the challenges. Between this avoidance of details and her staying out late and drinking, there was enough for Sky to get worried.

"Better get going for school, the chauffeur will be here any minute," Kat said.

"Right. Thanks for the pancakes, they were delicious," Sky said as he left the table.

As Sky finished his preparations for school, some ideas came to him that he wanted to write in his journal. He kept a daily journal in which he made notes about his experiences and kept track of goal-oriented actions. The journal served for quick, spontaneous entries when ideas suddenly popped up. He grabbed his journal and jotted down these thoughts: Kat was concerned about the new store launch, he felt certain of that. There was some factor not going according to plan, but he was not sure exactly what. She was constantly tired, looked worn down, and was drinking too much. Her mood was on edge, and she avoided being honest with him. She was clearly not getting enough sleep, and he remembered his grand-dad Vince saying good sleep was necessary for great performance, bringing essential rejuvenation. His mom's current downward spiral was alarming. The conclusion of this journal entry was to be patient and supportive of his mom. Writing these things down would be a reminder to keep these two qualities at the forefront during their interactions.

The downstairs door buzzer rang, and Sky knew the chauffeur was waiting to drive him to school. He stuffed the journal into his school backpack and hurried out. Kat was standing by the open door. Sky reached up to kiss her goodbye, and then left for school.

THIRTEEN

SKY SETTLED INTO the passenger seat next to the chauffeur. It was his habit to sit next to the driver so they could have conversations more easily. The two had developed a friendly relationship and shared about their lives during the trips to school.

"How are you doing in the tryouts for the select team?" asked the chauffeur.

"Pretty well. I think my pitching is close to top form now. Coach is noticing, and it's a real good chance that I'll be chosen," Sky said.

"That's great! You deserve being chosen; you've been so diligent in keeping up with practice and perfecting your skills. That's what it takes, and I'm certainly rooting for you."

Sky heard the sincerity in the chauffeur's voice and knew he meant every word. He smiled at the middle-aged man and nodded.

"Thanks. I do appreciate your support a lot. I'm working hard for the place on the select team."

The chauffeur pulled up to the school entrance, let Sky out and said goodbye and good luck. Sky saw his buddies and walked over to join them. As they entered the school hallway on the way to class, they talked about the upcoming chemistry test.

"Boy, I wish that chemistry test was further off," said one friend.

"Yeah, it's going to be brutal," chimed in another.

"I don't think I'll ever be ready no matter how far off it is," moaned a third friend.

"Hey, guys," Sky retorted, "one battle at a time. Right now, I've got to focus on my pitching for the select team tryouts tomorrow. Chemistry will have to wait a few more days, maybe *then* I can worry about passing the test."

As he walked, Sky pulled out his journal and, juggling the backpack around, found a pen, and jotted an entry about studying for the chemistry test. His buddies noticed what he was doing and made a few jokes about how writing this down was as good as 10 hours of studying. Sky grinned wryly. He was used to this kind of jibing from his friends. He knew it was all in good fun, and they meant no harm.

"Just kidding," one friend said just to be sure Sky didn't take it wrong.

"No problem," Sky replied. "You guys never make fouls on me. I know you're in my court and understand that the tryouts tomorrow are the most important thing now. I've got to stay present in the moment and focus on the task in front of me. Today and tomorrow, baseball, the next day, chemistry."

"That's for sure," the same friend said. "Did you know that Doug will be trying out tomorrow to make pitcher in the select team?"

Sky went silent for a few moments at hearing this news. Doug was his main competitor as a pitcher—actually, more like an arch-enemy due to the animosity that had developed between them. As far as Sky knew before, Doug had decided not to compete for pitcher in the select team. His pitching was not accurate enough in Sky's opinion. But maybe Doug had been practicing hard and improving his skills. This troubled Sky, and he did not welcome the challenge.

Before his mind could run away with creating scenarios in which Doug was besting him for the pitching position, Sky took several deep breaths to master his mind. This was a technique that Kat had taught him to regain control of emotional reactions. He concentrated on the deep breathing as he felt air enter through his nose, go deep into his lungs, and slowly exhale through his mouth. After taking four deep breaths, he felt calm.

Now he could apply his grand-dad's "180-Degree Mindset Model" and change his thoughts from negative to positive. According to the model, when you are harboring self-defeating thoughts, it's critical to switch these to the opposite pole before they settle in and take over. He had used it many times, always with good results.

"It's fine," he replied to his friends. "Doug is a good player, and he's probably been working on his game, like I've been doing. That's only natural. But I'm a better player. Not to worry."

Sky's focus and determination were evident in his steady, firm voice. His buddies nodded, and one clapped him on the back.

"We're with you, bud!"

"You're the best," they said, voices joined in a supportive chorus.

The school day seemed to drag on endlessly to Sky. When lunch came, he met his buddies again for quick bites, then went back to afternoon classes. It was hard for Sky to concentrate; all he could think about was the final practice for the tryouts after school. At last, the bell rang to end his final class, and Sky bolted from his desk to get ready for practice. He geared up quickly and soon was on the mound, ready to pitch.

Inning after inning, Sky threw his best pitches repeatedly, striking out most batters. His pitching was dominating. When he came up to bat, he made several base hits and turned some into doubles by his impressive speed running. He even stole two bases, to the loud cheers of his team. When in the dugout, he kept encouraging his teammates, infusing them with his enthusiasm. Team spirit and confidence were running high. The coach could not fail to notice how Sky was a natural leader, as well as a very talented player.

As Sky took the mound to pitch his last inning, previously determined by the coach, he glanced at the dugout and saw Doug sneering at him, drawing a finger across his throat. There was no mistaking Doug's meaning; he signaled the end of Sky's pitching and implied that HE would be the pitcher instead. It was time for pitchers to switch during practice, and Doug would be throwing for the last few innings.

Sky took a few more deep breaths and set his view on the batter, concentrating on his next pitch. He threw his fastest and most accurate sinker and struck out the batter amid cheers as he retired to the side. Sky still felt irritated by Doug's aggressive gesture. It was hard to keep this challenge from getting under his skin. Doug threw well but not close to how dominating Sky's performance had been. Sky felt good about his chances of gaining the starting pitcher position for the select team.

After practice, Sky was driven home by one of his friend's moms. After letting himself into the condo, he tossed his backpack on the floor, clicked on the PlayStation and flopped onto his bed, waiting for it to boot up. He didn't expect his mom home for some time and knew he'd be on his own for dinner. Unable to get involved with the PlayStation, he stared up at the ceiling, thinking about how stressed his mom had been lately. He felt certain most of her stress was over the new store opening and wondered how he might be helpful. Before long, he switched off the PlayStation and grabbed his journal to write down the results of his brainstorming. Ideas were swirling through his head, and he jotted them down rapidly.

After a few minutes, he landed on the idea of influencer marketing on TikTok, a social media channel all the kids were talking about. He liked the flexibility and instant appeal the app offered for creating and sharing short music, dance, and comedy videos, even providing space for lip-sync. Everyone could create these videos and share their creative expressions widely. It could snowball into a real social happening. Sky liked the idea of using TikTok to promote his mom's new store. He circled it among his list of brainstormed ideas for further development.

Realizing that he was hungry, Sky went to the kitchen and warmed up a frozen pizza for dinner. Though pizza was a frequent meal, he still enjoyed it every time. After cleaning up, he played video games for a while just to unwind before bed. Tired from his intense day at school and baseball practice, he fell asleep long before Kat came home.

FOURTEEN

GLARING BRIGHTNESS JOLTED Sky from sleep the next morning as Kat turned on the bedroom lights. Smiling at his sleepy grimace, she told him that breakfast would be ready soon, and to get his morning routine done. When she left the room, he rolled out of bed in his typical fluid motion onto the floor, did a set of pushups and calisthenics, reviewed his goals written on the whiteboard, and looked over his journal notes to recapture thoughts about both his long-term and day's goals. This was Sky's version of The Championship Hour that he learned from his mom and his grand-dad. He knew that how you spent the first hour of the day prepared you to win and set patterns. Exercise was important to Sky, but reflecting and reviewing goals were equally significant.

After a quick wash-up, he headed to the kitchen, drawn by the aroma of bacon and eggs. Once Sky had a chance to wolf down half of his breakfast, Kat inquired about the baseball tryouts for the select team today.

"It's the big day," Kat said. "Are you ready? How're you feeling about it?"

"I'm feeling really excited," Sky replied, "and also pretty nervous."

"Well, that's perfectly normal. Actually, it's good to feel a little nervous. It would be strange if you were not nervous, and that gives you an edge. You can channel that energy to your advantage. You just need to stay on top of it, not let it chip away your confidence." Kat smiled and winked at her son. "You've got all the tools to do that. Grand-dad prepared you to win."

Sky smiled back and chuckled to himself, since those very thoughts were his own, too.

"Mom, I had an idea last night that could help out with your new store launch," Sky said. He told her about attracting social influencers using TikTok, and ways they might be drawn into creating videos featuring her athletic products. Kat perked up at the idea, her eyes brightening. She told Sky this approach had a lot of potential; she liked it and would take it up with her marketing team.

"Thanks for taking the time to come up with ideas to help the store launch," Kat said. "I know today's tryouts must be at the forefront of your mind. But I know you're ready, I've watched how much you've practiced and prepared for it. I'll be your biggest fan there to cheer you on at the tryouts."

Sky beamed at his mom. He always loved it when she came to watch him play.

"Thanks, Mom, it means a lot to me," he said. "Both things, actually." She nodded at the acknowledgement of her praise for his TikTok idea.

The downstairs buzzer signaled that the chauffeur was ready at the door to take Sky to school. He gave Kat a quick goodbye kiss, grabbed his backpack and gear, and hurried out. Sky sat in his usual front seat passenger location, and the chauffeur began making conversation, inquiring again about the tryouts later that day. Sky politely told the chauffeur that it was important to stay focused on the tryouts, and he wanted to listen to the coach's practice tapes on audio.

"I can't imagine how you could be more ready," the chauffeur remarked.

"You can always be more ready," Sky replied. "It's a matter of intense focus and single-minded concentration. Listening again to coach's advice will help me increase my edge."

With that, Sky put in his earbuds and started the audio file, looking straight ahead. The chauffeur smiled, shaking his head and laughing inwardly as he thought how crazy this kid was for being overly dedicated to baseball, which was just a game, after all. But he left Sky to focus on listening and drove silently the rest of the way.

Maintaining his singular focus, Sky kept the earbuds in during lunch and avoided conversation with his buddies. They understood and didn't try to interrupt him. He endured the interminable afternoon classes until, finally, the bell rang.

Time to go. Tryout day. Sky's heart was pounding as he geared up and went to the bullpen for warm-ups. As the pitches soared from his hand, peace descended upon him. He knew he was ready for this. It was a state of mind his grand-dad called "Getting into the Zone." After a short time, Doug joined Sky in the bullpen to warm up. When Sky glanced at him, Doug again drew his finger across his throat. But before Doug could finish the gesture, Sky looked away, pointedly ignoring him. From the corner of his eye, Sky caught Doug's deflated expression and could tell his rival was pissed off.

As the tryouts began, Sky looked at the bleachers and was reassured to see Kat sitting in her usual area, right behind the catcher. They exchanged smiles, and Kat gave a thumbs-up. Sky started pitching, and everyone watching was amazed. He pitched nine straight strikes, retiring the first three batters handily. His next three times at bat, he hit sneaky ground balls and flew around the bases, making a double and even one triple. The shouts of the crowd watching the tryouts acknowledged his speed, almost beating some of the fastest kids trying out. His pitching stayed consistent and dominating.

Doug was pitching for the opposite team and doing well, though not at Sky's level. Toward the end of the tryout game, Sky was on third base waiting to sprint home from the bunt that his team's batter was about to make. It was a good bunt toward the first base line, giving Sky clear passage to home plate. As Sky was running home, Doug, as pitcher, took the spot of the catcher, who was chasing the ball. Doug positioned himself over home plate, ready to take the catcher's toss and tag Sky. Rapidly gaining speed, Sky took a slide into home plate. Doug saw this maneuver and lowered his knee just in front of Sky, forcing Sky's face to collide into Doug's leg.

It was an illegal move, and the crowd was booing. Kat leaped to her feet with a scream. As the dust lifted, Sky rose with his nose bleeding, bright red splotches on his shirt. Sky immediately leapt at Doug and shoved him hard, making him stagger. Doug came back swinging, and Sky ducked while sending a knee sharply into Doug's groin. This dropped Doug like a rock. As Doug lay groaning on the ground, Sky kicked dust into his face to humiliate him.

The umpire came running up to separate the combative boys. He yelled at them both about unsportsmanlike behavior, threw them out of the game, and ordered them to leave at once for the principal's office.

FIFTEEN

IN THE PRINCIPAL'S office, Kat was on her feet yelling at the gray-haired, middle-aged man. Obviously accustomed to such parental outbursts, the principal sat calmly behind his desk, hands folded over his rotund belly. Sky was seated in a chair close by, holding a bloodied rag to his nose and becoming increasingly embarrassed.

"You should have seen the whole thing!" Kat fumed. "Doug started it all; it's entirely his fault. You can't blame Sky for defending himself. It was illegal and dangerous! Look, Sky's nose is still bleeding."

"Yes, Ms. Von Slyke, I know what Doug did was illegal. However, Sky's reaction and counterattack were unacceptable. Coach puts heavy emphasis on being good sportsmen; on taking insults in stride. That's the mark of maturity in a player," said the principal in his most conciliatory voice.

"But my son was injured!" Kat insisted in a shrill voice. "His nose might be broken! Doug is to blame; he's the one who was a poor sportsman."

"That is so, and I'm sorry for your son's injury. Yes, Doug was wrong, but so was Sky. They both bear responsibility for the altercation. Doug is also suffering a painful injury from what Sky did to him."

Kat kept badgering the principal for a while, but he did not budge from his position. Sky looked with pleading eyes at his mom, silently asking her to stop. Finally, her head of steam wore down, and she fell silent.

"Let's discuss this like reasonable adults, Ms. Von Slyke," the principal continued. "Both boys violated the rules, and both will suffer the consequences. Sky will get detention for a week, and Doug will get detention for two weeks because he initiated the fight. Coach will decide when—and if—the boys can return to the team. Sky will be expected to continue his schoolwork while serving in detention, along with the rest of his classmates. This should not affect his progress in school as long as he completes assignments as required."

Turning to Sky, the principal concluded with, "I hope your nose heals well and isn't broken, Sky. But, take this lesson to heart. Don't get carried away by reactive emotions. Those will not serve you well, regardless of your career choice."

On the car ride home, Kat kept fuming about how unfairly Sky had been treated. She repeated her litany of Doug's offenses and insisted that he should be expelled.

"Wait, Mom," Sky mumbled through his nose rag. The bleeding had almost stopped now. "It was kinda my fault, too, you know. I engaged in that fight with Doug, and I shouldn't have."

Kat would not have any part of Sky taking the blame. She ran through the entire sequence again.

"That's not so, Sky! You know Doug started it; that was completely clear to everyone watching. You heard their booing. And most people are aware that Doug is a known bully. No one would fault you for acting in your own self-defense when Doug started swinging. You had to stop him, or he would have destroyed your face. You had to put him to the ground, and you really did it effectively."

"All you say is true, Mom," Sky replied slowly. "But stop and think it over. If I hadn't reacted, if I hadn't pushed Doug, then his illegal move to put his knee into my face would have led to natural consequences. Everyone saw what he did, and the umpire and coach would have put disciplinary actions into effect. Doug would have been suspended from the team and sent to detention—just Doug. But by fighting back, I made myself a party to the misbehavior. I put myself in a position to face the consequences for my actions."

Kat started a quick defensive response, but Sky just put out his hand to stop her.

"Think, Mom," he said gravely. "Remember the rules of sportsmanlike conduct. Remember what you've taught me about controlling emotional reactions. It's what

Grand-dad calls the Inner Game, the inside-out process where your thoughts and feelings lead to actions. When I reacted violently, I was giving away my power to Doug. Even if my body was assaulted, I didn't have to give in to anger. No one can take your mind away unless you give it to them."

That pulled Kat up short. She fell into a thoughtful silence.

"And one more thing," Sky said. "I don't feel good about kicking dust in Doug's face after he was down . . . that was insulting."

It was too much wisdom for Kat to take, and her mother tiger instincts flared.

"Sky, he deserved every single thing you did to him!" Kat exclaimed. "I was proud of how you put that mean bully into his well-deserved place on the ground. Great techniques! Doug will think twice before he takes you on again."

Sky gave a rueful smile to himself. You couldn't ask for a more loyal mother who would fight to the finish for your rights, especially when she thought someone violated them. He couldn't help but admire her passion and devotion.

"OK, OK, you've definitely got a few points," he acquiesced. "Thanks for your unwavering support. I love you, Mom."

Kat reached over and patted Sky's leg, shooting him a big smile.

"Me too," she murmured. "I'm always in your camp; you know that."

Sky could sense that his mom was calming down. His acknowledging her strong feelings was helping them dissipate. They finished the ride home in silence, each submerged in their own thoughts.

Sky knew deep inside that he was sorry for what he did to Doug. He realized his reactions were a mistake and had led to trouble for him, which could have been avoided. Maybe he would tell Doug that he was sorry in the future, at least apologize for kicking dust in his face. But, he wasn't sure if that was the best approach with a bully. He would wait and see.

Most of all, Sky was troubled about the consequences for his making the select team. He was unsure now if he was going to make the team at all, despite his dominating performance during the tryouts.

SIXTEEN

WHEN SKY AND Kat entered their condo, Sky headed straight toward his room. Kat put a hand on his shoulder to catch his attention.

"Are you OK?" she asked.

Sky turned to his mom and nodded, eyes lowered.

"Do you want to talk some more, process things?" Her concern showed clearly in her eyes.

"No, not just yet," Sky replied. He glanced at her but quickly looked away. He was struggling to stay in control of his emotions. "Now I'd like just to rest and have a little time alone."

"Sure," Kat said. "See you later at dinner. Have a good rest, and get that bloody nose cleaned a bit more."

Sky nodded and turned away, heading down the hall to his room. Kat went toward the kitchen to begin dinner.

Once inside his room, Sky locked the door. He really did not want his mom coming in right then. He stood, staring at his goal whiteboard on the back of the door. The goal he had written there, to become a major league baseball pitcher, loomed huge in bold black letters that seemed to leap toward him from the white surface. He squeezed his eyes closed to try to stop the hot tears welling up inside. His mind was clamoring with critical thoughts about how stupid he had been to get in the fight with Doug, how he probably had damaged his chances to make the select team, how his reputation was tarnished, how he might even have jeopardized his major league prospects.

Sky struggled against letting himself go down this path of self-sabotage. It was hard to resist feeling sorry for himself, beating up on himself, feeling hopeless. But he knew that surrendering to this path was a big mistake. He knew better; he had been taught the dangers of self-pity and how that sapped the energy and twisted the mind, leading to defeat. He would not give in. He would summon his strength and determination and take another path, one more positive and self-affirming.

He wiped the tears from his eyes, took out his journal, and sat on the bed as he opened it on his lap. He began practicing the technique his mom had taught him, called LSGT. Kat's father first introduced her to this method, and she found it such a useful strategy that she passed it on to her son. It was very effective in approaching life's challenges, and Sky had used it several times before. In his journal he wrote the acronym and each letter's meaning to refocus his mind:

L – Learn. We learn from our experiences, other people's experiences, and teachings by coaches. In any experience or teaching, ask what you are supposed to learn. Look for what opportunities these bring to learn something that could be helpful in tough times. You learn from others' successes and failures. In this process, you become the observer.

S – Study. We study these experiences or teachings by replaying our past performances in this area. By studying, you search for a deeper meaning that may lie beneath the surface. New patterns or obstacles might appear that help make additional connections. Keep delving deeper for what you're supposed to learn here. Difficulties are not meant to take you out of the game, but to make you better at it.

G – Grow. We grow from what we learn and study about these experiences and teachings. They are lessons toward mastery, making you better at what you do. You develop new beliefs, strategies, and skills through this examination of past performance. It may appear that you've failed, but it is only the ground for growth. If you never fail, you never learn and grow.

T – Train. Training is the process through which we put new strategies, beliefs, and skills into action. As these new capacities are implemented and repeated, you put in place a new set of habits. Regular, consistent repetition is essential to developing habits that replace older, less-effective ones. As you train and establish new habits, you move into the next level of mastery. This new plateau in the climb toward peak performance actually positions you for the next failure. When this failure or challenge happens, you begin the LSGT process all over again. It seeds the subsequent level of mastery. With this model, you'll never look at setbacks and failures in the same way. This is the evolution of growth.

Next, Sky applied each concept of the acronym to his current challenge. What could he learn from his reactive fight with Doug? How would he study the details and dynamics of this event to more deeply understand it? Where could he find ways to grow from this experience? And once he had completed these steps, how would he put his new beliefs and strategies into action, training himself to make them habits?

Learn. Pulling his concentration inside, he examined each step of the brewing confrontation with Doug and the feelings these evoked. He asked himself what he could learn from each step, striving to remain neutral and in observation mode. He needed to see what these experiences were teaching him. The gesture Doug had made of cutting his throat was the inciting incident at the previous day's practice. Sky had ignored it then, so why did he feel so provoked on tryout day? Of course, the stress level was higher because it was the actual game that would decide who made the team. From this, he learned the importance of staying aware of how stress shortened his fuse; to factor that in and be extra vigilant. This put him into observer mode. He learned the hard lesson of facing the consequences of one's actions. Because he'd let his awareness slip and lost control of his feelings, he might have compromised his goals. It was far better to prevent mistakes than to remedy the results.

Study. Sky delved more deeply into just how the chain of events had happened, and what he could have done differently. First, he should have acknowledged to himself that Doug's throat-cutting gesture really irritated him. If he'd felt that emotion fully, it would be released and not brewing inside. Next, he could have used stress-reducing techniques such as deep breathing and affirmations for several days before the tryouts. That would have decreased his trigger reactions and lengthened his fuse. Even in the heat of the game, while sliding into home plate, he needed to maintain greater awareness. He admitted how hard that was to do; only by repeated practice would it become a habit. The flare of anger that erupted after Doug's knee hit his face was pure gut instinct. Could such primal reactions really be controlled? He thought it was probably possible, but required more study and self-control disciplines. Maybe he couldn't have stopped from kneeing Doug, but he could have surely avoided kicking dirt in his face once he was down. Even that might have reduced the consequences he now had to face.

Grow. Sky could see a lot of growth opportunities in this experience. He needed to include stress reduction techniques in his everyday routine, not just when something was challenging him. And especially when facing a challenge, he should be more diligent using these techniques. He needed to become the observer more regularly. When things were irritating him, he would bring them out in the open, recognize they were affecting him and find ways to dissipate these feelings. In this situation, he might have talked with his mom about how much Doug irritated him, and why he felt so strongly against bullying. Kat would be understanding and supportive and encourage him to use the methods he had already learned. His buddies were also sources of support and unburdening his emotions. He had resources; his growth path was to utilize them regularly. He could also grow by examining his own aggressive impulses, understanding their source and what set them off, and finding healthy ways to change them. Both his mom and grand-dad were skilled at this.

Train. Once Sky had completed the study and grow parts of the process, he knew that training was essential to anchor his new beliefs, skills, and strategies. He would take every opportunity to put them into practice, moving him toward the next level of mastery. Using new abilities daily would turn them into habits that he could rely upon, habits that became automatic. This was the evolution of his growth and would help him never to see obstacles or failures the same way. As his grand-dad said, each new training brought mastery of the next level, which then led toward the next failure, setting up the entire LSGT cycle again.

After completing the LSGT exercises and writing down his responses, Sky felt calm and again in his center. He was encouraged that he would get through this challenge and even benefit from what he had learned by growing toward greater mastery. After washing his face, careful to wipe away all residual blood from his nose, he felt ready to join Kat for dinner.

SEVENTEEN

KAT WOKE A few minutes before her alarm was set to go off at 4:30 a.m. She had not slept well, and her mind was already racing, sorting through bizarre dreams as well as the even more disorienting events happening in her non-dream life. A thousand thoughts competed inside her mind, each clamoring for her attention. There were the numerous details surrounding the new store launch. She was still trying to come to grips with her father's cancer. Now Sky's baseball career seemed in trouble. She was worried that he wouldn't be chosen for the select team and how that could impact his future. Her own lack of control troubled her. She recalled the recent unpleasant episodes due to drinking too much. It wasn't like her to over-react like that in social situations, or to drink in excess.

As Kat lay in bed, stewing over all the things that seemed beyond her control, the alarm sounded and jarred her into action. She quickly dressed in workout clothes and went to the gym. At least she could control her workout routine, and it usually settled her mind. This morning, however, she couldn't even get a good sweat going. Try as she would, she simply wasn't able to focus. After several attempts to use sheer willpower to force her body into the machine routines, she realized it just wasn't happening. With a sigh, she gave up trying and went to the locker room, where she sat in the sauna contemplating. The whirling thoughts in her mind prevented any effective problem-solving. After a while she just sat, releasing her body to the hot, steamy sauna.

At work, Kat was kept busy dealing with endless questions and issues her staff needed addressed. She went through the day on autopilot, appearing on the surface to be her usual in-command self, but inside was disoriented and scattered. Out of the blue, she got a text from a good friend, Vicky, who wanted to have lunch. Though it seemed a bit strange to Kat, since Vicky almost never wanted to take up her lunch break by going out, it was also a relief. Kat could use a friend just now, someone she could vent to who was a sympathetic listener. Kat agreed and set off shortly to meet her friend.

Kat pulled her Mercedes into the parking lot of a local mall with several good restaurants. She felt excited to see Vic after several weeks with no contact. After parking, she headed toward their designated meeting place at the mall entrance, where she nearly bumped into her friend. Kat and Vic were complementary opposites. Both were tall, although Kat had two inches on Vic, vigorous and well-muscled. Kat's tawny hair, fair skin, blue eyes, and slender, lean frame contrasted with Vic's tight black curls, chocolate skin, ebony eyes, and generous curves. They both smiled widely and hugged, standing close at the side of the street to chat a little before deciding on a restaurant.

After their greetings, Kat admitted that she had been on edge recently.

"Lots going on in my world," Kat said. "Things have been challenging, and I'm so glad for an opportunity to have a good talk with a friend."

"I know the feeling," Vic responded. "I've got some pretty important news to share with you, too."

"Well, let's go in and get talking," Kat quipped with more vigor than she felt.

They both started walking across the street in the parking lot toward the main mall entrance, still engrossed in conversation. A car suddenly swung around the corner of the next parking aisle heading right toward them. Tires screeched as the driver braked hard to avoid hitting them, veering sharply to the side. Both women pulled up and sidestepped, but had little room to maneuver.

The car driver rolled down his window, face red and fuming with anger. He started yelling at them through the car window.

"You dumb bitches! Can't you watch where you're walking? Damn women, no common sense, can't pay attention, gabbing all the time."

Kat was incensed and couldn't control her reaction.

"Screw you! You're supposed to watch out for pedestrians!" she yelled back.

The man's face got even redder and his eyes bulged as if they might explode out of their sockets. He stuck his head farther out the window and pointed a finger at Vic.

"You and your idiot friend don't have no right to jaywalk in front of me. Get your asses the hell out of my way before I run you down."

"Up yours!" Kat retorted back.

"Shut your own filthy mouth! Think you're better'n me, fancy pants?" the driver sputtered, spittle flying as he began foaming at the mouth.

The driver's insults lit a fire inside Kat. She was wearing her usual chic outfit, designer jeans, and tailored silk blouse, with expensive platform boots that had heavy soles and reinforced toes. Impulsively she lashed out by kicking the nearest front door of his car, causing a small dent. For good measure, she kicked the same place a second time, deepening the dent.

"F**king asshole!" Kat spat at the man. "What a hoser! Total shithead!"

The driver looked as if he might have a stroke, let out a roar, and threw open the car door. Both Kat and Vic stepped back at his threatening demeanor, fists balled, shaking his arms violently at them. The man was middle-aged and burly, with gray-streaked hair and sunburned light skin, dressed in worn jeans, T-shirt, and dirty tennis shoes. His gray eyes were narrowed in a killer squint and appeared glazed over as though he was in a trance.

"F**king bitch you're gonna pay for that!" he yelled, more spittle propelled violently from his lips. "Snooty spoiled rich brat! You're gonna regret what you done. I got my rights, too, and you're up against'm!"

EIGHTEEN

THE FURIOUS MAN lunged quickly toward Kat, and before she could move out of his reach, he pushed her. She twisted away to avoid the man's shove and used his momentum to propel him forward, slamming him against the car's open door, which shut under his weight. His head hit the doorframe hard, making a loud thunk. Now even more furious, shaking his head in an attempt to clear it, he took a wild swing at Kat. She blocked his arm with hers and stomped sharply on his foot. Yowling like a wild animal, he started jumping around in circles on the other foot. Taking advantage of his being unbalanced, Kat shoved him hard, and he fell to the ground. As Kat tried to move away, he reached out and grabbed her leg, tackling her into the side of the car. Kat kicked hard to release her foot and struggled to stay upright, holding onto the car roof.

Vic was screaming, freaking out over the fight. When she saw that Kat couldn't free her leg from the man's grip and that he was dragging her down, Vic entered the fray, trying to separate them. She pulled against the man's arm but wasn't able to make him let go, so she kicked him hard in the side. He yelled and released Kat's leg, raising both arms to cover his face. Kat stepped away and tried to grab Vic, who was preparing for another kick to the man's head.

A mall security guard came running over holding a Taser. Vic was closest to the guard, so he aimed the Taser and stunned her. Kat screamed as she watched her friend crumple to the ground. With a burst of fury, she leapt at the guard and delivered a hard punch to the side of his face, causing blood to splatter from his nose. Unprepared for this attack, the surprised guard was sent sprawling to the ground. Kat kicked the Taser out of his hand and started yelling at him.

"Why'd you do that? It's the stupid guy's fault; he attacked us! He started it!"

The security guard rolled away from Kat and staggered to his knees, reaching around for his Taser. Kat dropped to her knees next to Vic, shaking her by the shoulders and desperately asking if she was OK. Her friend still appeared dazed and unable to reply. During the short time that Kat, Vic, and the security guard were distracted, the man got up, sprang back into his car, and was quickly speeding away.

"Hey! He's getting away, that bastard that started everything!" Kat yelled. She watched as the man turned with screeching wheels and exited the mall parking lot, disappearing down the street.

Vic was moaning softly, her eyes fluttering. Kat held her and gently lifted her head, turning attention to her friend.

The security guard had recovered his Taser and risen to his feet when another security guard came running out. The two security guards told Kat to stand aside and lifted Vic, supporting her as the Taser effects began to wear off. Each guard gripped one woman's arm and shoved them toward the mall entrance. A small crowd had gathered to watch the excitement.

"We're taking you into custody, to the mall security office," the second guard said.

"It's not our fault!" Kat insisted. "That guy, the one that just drove off, he started it. He almost ran us down and then cursed at us and attacked us!"

"Just come along quietly, ma'am," said the guard. "We'll get your statements at the security office."

"No, really, we're not the ones at fault!"

"You caused a disturbance," the guard replied, "and assaulted a mall security guard. You'll need to explain things at the office. We may have to call the police. Come quietly now."

Within minutes, both Kat and Vic were ushered into the mall security office, placed in a closed room and informed that the security supervisor would be there to question them soon. Sitting on hardback chairs next to each other, Kat put an arm around Vic's shoulders and asked how she was feeling. Vic shook her head, murmuring that she still felt dazed.

Kat also felt shocked. She couldn't believe what had just happened, and all so quickly. This wasn't like her, getting in a public brawl and taken into custody by security guards. Sure, she got angry and flared up, but not like this. This was something else, and something was terribly wrong. Now she felt scared, ashamed at her uncontrollable reaction and violent behavior. She was unraveling right before her own eyes, making a public display and drawing her friend into trouble with her.

Vic started crying quietly beside Kat as they sat in the stark holding room of the security office. Kat tried to say something comforting, but Vic simply put up a hand, halting Kat's words. Vic shook her head again and slowly gained composure, wiping away tears. They sat in silence for a while, but when Kat started to say something, Vic put up her hand again.

"Don't say anything, Kat," Vic said softly. "Just listen to me. I want you to hear what I'm telling you. Something is going terribly wrong inside of you. This fighting . . . losing control of your anger, jumping at the guy and attacking him like you did. . .. there's something else going on. Your reaction isn't just about this one event; it's deeper. What's bothering you so badly that it gets you to react this way?"

Kat was taken aback. Vic's words made it painfully clear that losing control so badly was tied to even deeper root issues. The stark reality of this, which she had been grappling to understand, was thrown into sharp focus.

"Look, Kat, let's admit that it's not easy being successful women and getting insulted by men," Vic continued. "We have immense hurdles to overcome. We've faced widespread discrimination for generations, having to struggle hard for every advance we achieve. You know that; you've contended with it your entire life and forged a successful career in the face of opposition. Nothing comes easily; we work hard for every little thing. These are just the facts. But over-reacting, losing control, and creating incidents is never going to help."

Kat nodded, looking straight ahead. Guilt was creeping over her for getting her friend into this predicament.

"One thing I've learned that keeps me on track through all these difficulties, especially as a Black woman," Vic continued, "is to let go of grievances and resentments. To maintain my center; that's how to navigate through these troubled waters. Whatever meanness and unfairness other people are hurling toward you is more about them than you. It's their own narrowness, personal fears, and learned prejudices. We need to rise above their shortcomings and practice kindness toward everyone. Anger and reactivity won't get us anywhere. You know this, Kat. Deep down, you know."

Kat was hanging her head down, fighting tears as she listened to Vic's words.

"You mentioned having problems, I'm aware of your new store, and that must be really demanding. But you're too volatile to handle stress effectively. If you can't keep in your center, things will rapidly get out of hand. I've never seen you act so combatively, actually getting into physical fights with that obnoxious man and the security guard. Kat, that's not like you. We've talked before about techniques to keep in balance. You must not be using them. Is there an opportunity in this situation for you to fix something inside? To understand what's bothering you so much that it gets you to react this way?"

Unable to find a good response, Kat sat in silence after Vic finished. What Vic said about Kat's life hit home. In flitting wisps of memory, some of her father's teaching passed through her mind. He told her that it's not what happens, but how you respond, that is most important. You can always be in control of how you respond; that is a choice you can make. "Success in life," Vince had said, "is an inside-out game. You must start on the inside, get things aligned there, and then you can keep your outside behaviors congruent with your values." However, it was now painfully obvious that Kat was failing miserably at this inner game.

Tears welled up in Kat's eyes, which she didn't try to stop. After a few long moments, she whispered to Vic.

"You're right. About everything. And I'm so sorry."

NINETEEN

IT WAS PERHAPS the most awkward day in Kat's recent life. She and Vic spent most of the afternoon in the holding room at the mall security office. At least they were given something to drink. That afternoon they had undergone interrogation by the security supervisor, who questioned both security guards and reviewed the surveillance cameras that caught the incident on video. The supervisor noted that it was clear from the video that the irate man had initiated the incident. After he got out of his car and attacked Kat, her actions were in self-defense. Vic getting shocked with the Taser by the security guard was an over-reaction, he concluded. Since the guard's nose was not broken and the bleeding had stopped, the mall would not make charges against Kat for assault.

Kat was grateful for the leniency shown to them by the security supervisor. She and Vic agreed that they would not take any actions related to the Taser incident, either.

Kat didn't say as much, but felt confident that a major reason for the accord was the mall management wanting to avoid adverse publicity and charges of mistreatment of two women. She and Vic certainly wanted to escape newspapers having a heyday with such stories. In all, they had spent nearly six hours in mall security custody. Any thoughts of having lunch were long gone.

During their time confined together, the two women hardly talked. Vic had said what she wanted to communicate to Kat while first inside the holding room. Besides, Vic seemed preoccupied with her own thoughts, and Kat felt too embarrassed and ashamed to break in. For her part, Kat had plenty of issues to mull over. She kept re-running the sequence of events leading up to the fight and examining where she had made mistakes. This only led her to feel depressed, since she knew better and had tools to keep her emotions under control. What was so wrong now that she couldn't access those tools? Her father's words about life being an inside-out game kept reverberating in her mind.

After being released, the two women hugged and promised to be back in touch soon, then left for their separate destinations. Kat made her way back to her car in the mall parking lot and headed home. She was thankful that Sky was spending the night at a friend's house. This spared her having to give difficult explanations about why she came home early. She was mortified about what Sky would think of her latest example of bad behavior, resulting in spending time in the security office. It was even worse than her drunken episodes.

Not able to deal with work that evening, Kat finished off a bottle of wine and slept in the next morning. When she arrived at her office, she found it in a dead panic. A passenger jet in the Middle East had been shot down, killing all 100 people on board. News sources had initially pointed to a terrorist attack and the response was a sudden sell off in the stock market. This was particularly bad news for Kat, since a good chunk of her wealth was tied up in public markets. She plunged into immediate worry about how this might impact liquidity of funds for the new store launch.

With everyone in the office looking to her for guidance, Kat tried not to panic and attempted to maintain a calm demeanor. She gave practical directions, such as keeping close tabs on official news releases, checking financial reports and watching the stock markets, and returning to their tasks to be accomplished that day. But, in light of everything she had been through over the past 24 hours, Kat was not in the best business mindset. She held the scheduled meeting to track marketing and publicity activities for the new store launch and offered a few constructive ideas. Several times she had to ask team members to repeat their questions, a most unusual behavior for their boss. A few exchanged concerned glances, but others were just relieved that she was not in attack mode, criticizing every little shortcoming or omission.

After the meeting, Kat hid away in her office, instructing her secretary to hold calls and tell anyone wanting her ear that she was involved in an important project, and to return later. Just for distraction, she began scrolling through Facebook. She absent-mindedly scanned several mundane posts by her friends, and even chuckled at a few amusing pictures and comments. Then she saw something that riveted her attention. It was a post several days ago made by Vic.

In the picture, Vic was in a clinic bed receiving an IV infusion. Vic wore a patient gown and had her hair covered with a cap. In her right arm was a needle with tubing for delivering the infusion from the bottle hanging on a stand beside the bed. Despite the serious appearance of this scene, Vic was smiling bravely. The caption for the picture said, "First day of chemo." In the accompanying post, Vic wrote that she was starting chemotherapy for breast cancer at a nearby chemo center. The cancer had been diagnosed two weeks earlier, and a course of chemotherapy planned that would span five months.

Kat gasped as her world was rocked to its very core. Reflexively, her hands flew to her heart, and she took several deep breaths. Vic had cancer! Why didn't she tell Kat before? Especially when they had been together just yesterday, but her friend had said nothing. Suddenly it dawned on Kat. This was why Vic had called to meet for lunch. Her friend was planning to share about the cancer then, but the fight Kat provoked had derailed it.

"Oh my God!" Kat moaned to herself. She dropped her face into both hands as tears stung her eyes. She had allowed herself to take a stupid course of action. Her uncontrolled reaction and its consequences had prevented her friend from talking about the major crisis she was facing. An important opportunity Kat might have had to be supportive, to show caring toward her good friend, was lost. Bitter regret seared Kat's emotions as she realized that, once again, she had given away her power to circumstances. She had failed at the inner game.

Immediately, she felt another flare-up of anger and resentment. What was the world doing to her? Why all this cancer entering her life again? First, her brother died years ago of leukemia, then her father diagnosed with advanced prostate cancer, and now one of her best friends had breast cancer.

And on top of that, the stock market crash was tanking her financial investments.

It was more than Kat's mind and emotions could take. She went numb, stunned into a state devoid of feeling, staring blankly at nothing.

TWENTY

HOW SHE MANAGED to get through the rest of the week was beyond Kat's comprehension. Some type of automatic survival mechanism kicked in, and she went through her daily activities, able to at least minimally function while hiding her true feelings from everyone—including Sky. She did call Vic by phone and have a good conversation, apologizing for the fight that interrupted their lunch. Kat let her good friend know how much she cared and that she wanted to offer support through this challenge. Vic was kind enough not to bring up her concerns about Kat's erratic behavior, simply thanking her for calling and promising they'd have that lunch soon.

By Thursday, Kat realized she needed to get away, to escape from her usual pressured life. She took Sky out of school Friday so they could spend a long weekend at her cabin by the lake in Banff. Sky was thrilled at the chance for them to be together in this secluded, peaceful setting and really catch up. They took her private jet before dawn that morning, then drove a rental car from the airport to Banff. During the drive up to the cabin, Kat was noticeably silent and only gave short responses to Sky's comments. He could tell she was preoccupied with something. It seemed to be eating away at her more than usual, and his emotional intelligence detected that there was a serious difficulty his mom was grappling with.

"Something unusual going on at work?" Sky asked.

"Ummm . . . nothing out of the ordinary," Kat replied.

"Are you worried about the stock market situation? You know, after that passenger airplane that was shot down?" He had read about the crash online.

Kat hesitated a moment and then decided that she could make a small admission of concern since he already knew about it.

"Well, yes, that's a big question at present," she said. "We don't know how it will affect the economy. Everyone is a little worried about that."

Sky waited to see if she would elaborate on how it might affect her business, but his mom kept her eyes on the road and offered no other information.

"It's really terrible, all those people killed in the crash," Sky said after a few minutes. "I heard that two were Canadians from Vancouver. I feel sad for their family and friends, and all the other people too."

"Uh-huh, it's tragic," Kat replied, but did not add more. Sky finally gave up, and they were silent the rest of the drive.

After they settled into the cabin, Kat suggested they go for a walk by the lake. The time was spent mostly walking quietly, apart from a few remarks about the birds and plants that were abundant in the area. Usually, these walks in nature allowed Kat to get settled into her inner self. Then she could access the power of being present, where enhanced awareness led to making better choices that produced better results. To her dismay, this time, she couldn't slip into the "gift of now" that being present brought.

At dinner that evening, Sky noticed that Kat didn't seem able to relax and let go of work. She kept checking her cellphone and responding to texts or emails, which prevented them from having an ongoing conversation. Finally, Sky raised an eyebrow as she picked up the cellphone again. Kat mumbled a slight apology.

"Sorry, it's just that I'm trying to keep up with the financial situation. A few questions to field from work, too."

Sky wasn't buying his mom's explanations. Now he felt certain something big was happening and she would not tell him about it. They had agreed to watch a movie after dinner, but even once they were curled up on the couch watching, the light of Kat's cellphone screen continued to absorb her attention. Sky squirmed uneasily, getting more irritated by his mom's behavior. The cabin at Banff was supposed to be a "no phone zone" where they would unplug from their everyday world and enjoy relaxing together. Sky had left his cellphone beside the bed in his room, which was the drill.

After the movie, Sky tried to engage Kat in their usual post-movie analysis and sharing their take on the story, acting, and cinematography.

"I found the lead character Frank a bit unconvincing," Sky observed. "He wasn't consistent in his attitudes and reactions. That last scene where he finally admitted his guilt just didn't ring true. He spent the whole film denying it, why the sudden turn-around?"

"Huh? Uh. . . guess I didn't notice that," Kat replied lamely. Actually, she could hardly remember anything about the movie.

"But his covering up was the major theme in the story! How could you miss that?"

"I was a little distracted," Kat said.

"Yeah, you sure were!" Sky retorted. "Checking your cellphone every two minutes. We're supposed to take cellphone breaks while we're at the cabin."

"I'm really sorry. A lot's been going on at work."

"Do you have any thoughts about the movie? What about that intense scene when Frank's business partner confronts him for skimming off profits and hiding it from everyone? They had built the business based on mutual honesty, and this was the ultimate betrayal. That was so well thought out and acted; I was really impressed."

Kat remained silent for several moments. She was clearly uncomfortable.

"I . . . I, uh, guess I was looking at my cellphone during that scene," she admitted.

"Mom, you weren't paying ANY attention to the movie!" Sky turned toward Kat and grabbed her cellphone, pulling it from her hand. "You're not supposed to be doing this! You know that using your cellphone during a movie just isn't right. We're here to be together and share! What's wrong with you?"

Kat stared in shock at her son. He hardly ever was so confrontational, and she knew he must be really upset. But he was right. She had not been present during the movie, and she had broken their cellphone agreement. Silently she realized how much she missed out in so many other ways by not being present lately.

TWENTY-ONE

SKY COULD FEEL something snap inside. He'd been able to remain calm and even offer his mom support through the past several weeks of her erratic behavior. She had hinted at excessive stresses at work, particularly with the launching of the new store. But, when she was stressed before, she was always more forthcoming with him, more willing to share details of her work life just as he shared his experiences at school, with friends, and with baseball.

He couldn't take her evasive and distancing actions anymore. Standing directly in front of Kat, he turned off the TV, and his eyes bored into hers.

"Mom, you've got to let me know what's going on! I know something's up, and it must be awful big because you are just not acting normal! Every time I ask, you try and say it's nothing out of the ordinary, but I know better. I can sense that there's a serious issue going on here. You've got to be more honest with me!"

Kat let out a little gasp and her eyes widened. Her son rarely confronted her like this and she could feel his anger. Before she could respond, Sky continued his barrage against her.

"You've been so distant lately. You're not keeping your word to me. I feel that you're hiding something, and that's not right. Just look at what's been going on—you're forgetting or skipping meals we'd planned to have together, you're coming home late almost every night, you always seem hyper-focused on work, and you're not spending time with me like we used to do. Mom, you're being a hypocrite. You're not doing all the things you taught me were important, were the right way to live and care about each other. Life isn't meant to be lived this way! Not the life that we want together, that we had before."

Sky's voice choked with emotion and he stopped, fighting back tears. He swallowed hard and tried to compose himself, but his words quavered as he said, "I miss my mom."

Kat heaved a big sigh and glanced away. It was clear to Sky that she was wrestling internally about what to say.

"Sky, I'm really sorry," Kat began, looking back into his eyes. "Work has been hellacious of late. Some crazy things are happening that demand my attention, and it's got to be my priority for a while. Things that are a real challenge for me to handle. It's not something I want to burden you with because there's nothing you can do to help. You wouldn't understand most of it, anyway."

Sky rolled his eyes at these timeworn and lame excuses.

"Try me," he retorted in a scathing tone of voice.

"Look, Sky, I just can't talk with you about these things at work," Kat replied. "There are some things that a child should not be burdened with. I'd be a bad parent if I unloaded it onto you. I'm trying to get things right, and it's not easy. Please make an effort to understand."

"But I want to share your burden," Sky insisted. "I know you, Mom, and something's not right. We're a team, just like in baseball. We always have each other's back. Like all the teamwork principles you and Grand-dad taught me. Remember the Rule of Three that he created? For real teamwork, you have to be on top of these three things: One, know yourself and your strengths and weaknesses; two, know and understand your teammates' strengths and weaknesses; three, know the strengths and weaknesses of the competition.

'Team players have to share and be honest with each other. Without that, they can't know each other's strengths and weaknesses. They need to let the team help carry the burden. No one player can do it all; teams increase each player's abilities by cooperating. Didn't you mean what you said? You and I, we're a team, and Grand-dad is our coach. Like any team, we have good and bad days—in life and in sports. But family supports each other like teammates do, no matter what. That's what you've always told me."

Kat was startled by Sky's remarks about being a team, and especially by bringing up his grandfather. Suddenly, remorse flooded through her. She had not checked on her father Vince for several days and wasn't updated about how his chemotherapy was going. Despite her promise to be with him when he started chemo, she'd begged off because of work pressure. Vince had been big-hearted enough to reassure her that he would be OK, saying a good friend was accompanying him. Though she had called him the day afterward and he said he was bearing up pretty well, she had let too many days slip by without a call.

Then the fight had happened at the mall when she was meeting Vic for lunch. And after that, the airplane was shot down over the Middle East and her office was in a panic over the stock market. She was thrown into a frenzy about her investments and how the government's freezing assets would affect her ability to finance the new store launch, which she had dangerously over-leveraged.

To cap off these disastrous events, she had learned on Facebook that her good friend Vic was diagnosed with breast cancer, and also undergoing chemotherapy treatment.

Kat felt utterly overwhelmed by the weight of all these events, and her shoulders sagged. Sky could see that she was emotionally on the brink, and he sat on the couch beside her, taking both her hands in his.

"Mom, you've got to tell me," he said softly. "I can handle it. I want to share your burden. Please let me know what's troubling you so much."

Almost horrified, Kat realized that she had not told Sky about his grandfather's cancer. It was something that he deserved to know, that he needed to know.

"OK. One of the biggest things causing me so much difficulty is your grandfather's health," she said. "There's no easy way to say this. He's got cancer. When the doctors discovered it, the cancer was pretty far advanced. They couldn't do surgery; he is going through a course of chemotherapy. It's likely he will need a second course. It's serious."

Sky felt his stomach clench, and a wave of nausea swept over him. He did not want to believe what he was hearing from Kat.

"Grand-dad has cancer? No, that can't be true!" Sky exclaimed. Memories of times with his grandfather flashed through his mind: sun glinting off mountain streams as they were fly-fishing, cheering on the Blue Jays together at games, wise lessons to live by, like, "Whatever you put your mind to you can accomplish." Vince always made Sky feel exceptional and full of abilities. His grandfather had been special in his life for as long as he could remember.

"I'm so sorry to tell you this," Kat murmured. "I can hardly believe it myself. I feel so devastated."

Sky sank back onto the couch and held his head between his hands.

"Oh, no, not Grand-dad," he moaned. "He's always been so strong. He'll get over this cancer, won't he?"

"We can hope and pray that he does," Kat said. She realized that Sky needed time to let this news settle in. She related to her son the sequence of events, her meeting with Vince, their discussion at his house, and the medical treatment plans. She knew that she should have told Sky sooner, both for his sake and for hers. She felt relief sharing with him, realizing he would be a source of support for her once he adjusted. The fact that Sky didn't reprimand her for the delay in telling him showed her son's maturity, for which she greatly admired him.

Sky listened carefully to his mom's description, taking it all in, letting this awful knowledge become the present reality. He blinked back tears and took her hands in his.

"We'll get through this, Mom. We're a team; we pick each other up."

Just then, her cellphone rang. They exchanged glances and Kat was almost going to ignore the call until she saw it was from Vince's good friend who accompanied him to chemotherapy. She informed Sky, who nodded for her to answer. After a short conversation, Kat tearfully shut off the phone and told Sky:

"Your grandfather is in the hospital, in the ICU. He's in critical condition."

TWENTY-TWO

THE FLIGHT BACK from Banff seemed unreasonably long. Kat and Sky didn't talk except for an occasional comment about how much longer until they got there. Both dozed fitfully part of the time. After arriving in Toronto in the early morning, they drove straight to the hospital where Vince was in the ICU. Kat had called ahead to let Vince's doctor know they were on their way, and he said he would meet them at the entrance to the critical care unit that morning. When they arrived and joined the doctor, his face was grave.

"This is an unexpected complication," the doctor said. "Vince appeared to be doing well with chemotherapy, when suddenly his body began to react violently. In a small number of people, the toxins in the chemo formula cause kidney or liver damage. Vince's kidneys have nearly shut down over the past two days. The damage appears irreparable, and his lab tests are steadily getting worse. It's too early to know for sure, but I need to prepare you for the worst."

"But . . . but he sounded fine the last time I talked to him," Kat said. "How could it happen so fast?"

"When this type of reaction takes place, the pathological processes make rapid progress," the doctor replied. "It's almost as if the body is at war against its own organs; in this case, the kidneys. We call it a fulminating autoimmune reaction. There is no completely effective treatment to stop the process once it begins. We're using steroid drugs to try and slow the immune system's hyper-reaction."

Kat asked a few more questions, unable to wrap her mind around her dad's condition. The doctor answered patiently but did not hold out much hope. He added that Vince's lungs were filling with fluid, a type of pneumonia, which was part of the syndrome. Even though dialysis was helping cleanse his bloodstream, it could not prevent this other complication. He ended by saying that Vince was relatively stable at the moment; conscious, but very weak.

Kat and Sky were allowed to enter Vince's ICU room, where they saw him lying in a hospital bed surrounded by machines. He had IV infusions going in both arms, a cardiac monitor that was softly beeping in time with his heartbeat, a urinary catheter and collection bag, and was receiving oxygen from a nasal cannula. He appeared pale with a grayish tinge to his skin, and his eyes were closed. They stood at one side of the bed, and Kat gently placed a hand on his shoulder.

"Dad? Dad, we're here. It's Kat and Sky."

Vince's eyelids flickered and then opened as he looked up at Kat, noticing that Sky stood beside her. He nodded and gave a weak smile.

"Come closer," Vince whispered. "It's hard to talk . . . not enough air."

"We came as soon as we heard," Kat said. "So sad to see you all hooked up like this. How are you doing?"

"Hanging in there," Vince replied, his voice breathy. "Not my favorite way to spend my time."

"I'll bet the food isn't too good, either," added Sky, trying to bring in some levity.

"Nowhere nearly as good as your cooking, Sky. Try to sneak in some decent food, will you?"

"I'll do my best," said Sky.

"What have you two been up to?" Vince asked.

They took turns talking about their quick trip to Banff. Sky briefly mentioned his select team tryouts, omitting anything about his fight and suspension. Kat glossed over things at work and only said a little about how much effort was being expended getting ready for the new store opening. They tried to keep conversation light, but it felt forced. It was a frightening situation; they had never seen Vince looking so weak and pale. All the ICU paraphernalia and the frequent checks by nurses intimidated them, adding to the aura of distress.

Vince was watching his daughter and grandson carefully under drooping eyelids. Although they were putting forward a calm front, he could sense that there was something wrong with Kat and Sky. Or perhaps something wrong between them. Even as his body systems were failing, his mind remained sharp and observant as ever. He knew his time with them would be limited, and wanted to get to the heart of things.

"Sky, there are some things I want to talk to your mother about," Vince said. "Could you give us a few minutes alone?"

"Sure, Grand-dad," said Sky, turning and leaving the room.

"Kat, I may not have much time left. " Sensing her uneasiness, he moved on quickly. "No, don't say anything, just listen. When I was young, early in life, I was wildly ambitious. I was relentless, always driving toward my goals, acquiring wealth, and I was very successful in my career. But all that sacrifice, ruthless discipline and one-pointed effort didn't make me happy. I was never truly happy in life until I married your mother, and you came along. You and your brother Max. That's when I learned that happiness comes from other kinds of success. From success in relationships, in family and friends, in living a good life, and loving others."

Vince stopped, coughing and running out of breath. Kat frowned in concern and patted his shoulder.

"Just rest, Dad," she said. "Don't burden yourself with talking."

"Kat, I need to say this now," Vince replied. "In case I don't get another chance. Wealth and success. I want to tell you what I've learned. There are many kinds of wealth—financial, career, friendships, family. You need success in all these areas, not just in career and finances."

Vince paused, locked eyes with his daughter, and continued.

"You are dead broke in a few of these areas. Take a good look at your life; really take some time to chart out where it's going. Do you want to end up where this road is taking you? I know you're successful in career and finances. But I see big problems in family and friendships. The choices you make now are critical in following the road to true happiness. Don't let it slip away from you."

Kat looked away, her emotions crashing in turmoil. Her dad was spot on about the problems in family and friendships. He just didn't know how precarious her financial situation and potential career fallout was now. Add that in, and her life was failing in every area.

When Vince spoke again, his voice was even weaker than before.

"Please send Sky in," he whispered. "I want some time alone with my grandson. Think about what I've just said."

Kat gave his shoulder a gentle squeeze, kissed his cheek, and turned away quickly so he would not see the tears welling in her eyes. She left the room to send Sky in and sat morosely in the waiting area, reflecting on exactly where she was in her life—no sugarcoating this time.

TWENTY-THREE

TWO DAYS LATER, Kat was called to the hospital at 6 a.m. because her dad was non-responsive. She and Sky had visited him the evening before and were warned that his condition was getting worse. Now he had slipped into a coma, and the doctor expected he would not last through the day. They were at Vince's bedside less than an hour later.

It broke Kat's heart to see her once-vigorous father lying so thin and pale, barely breathing. Although she tried talking to him, it was obvious that he could not hear. Sky stood on the opposite side of the hospital bed, grasping his grandfather's bony hand, shocked by how cold it felt. Mother and son kept vigil until Vince peacefully passed away, breath gradually dwindling to soft gasps before stilling.

During the few hours of their vigil, both Kat and Sky had whispered goodbyes to Vince. They repeated how much they loved him and would miss his uplifting presence in their lives. They made promises to keep him always in their hearts and never forget everything he had taught and given to them. Tears came and went until both settled into quiet numbness, each holding one of Vince's hands, transfixed by the mystery of a soul departing from its body.

After the doctor pronounced Vince's death, he took them aside to discuss arrangements for the funeral. Kat responded mechanically to set the process in motion. Sky just stood beside his mom, staring blankly across the room. When finished with what could be arranged for now, they made one final visit for a last farewell, gathered Vince's belongings, and went out to their car to drive home.

It was Monday afternoon. Kat could hardly believe that only three days ago, she and Sky had left for the cabin in Banff for a weekend of relaxation and fun. That hadn't turned out so well, she recalled. They had argued and been interrupted by the phone call from Vince's doctor. Now they had lost a father and grandfather in a whirlwind of events that left them stunned.

Both were somber and couldn't find anything to say during the drive back to their condo. Kat had turned her cellphone completely off, something she had not done in years. She did not want any texts or calls from work. She had not even let her assistant know that she was not coming to the office. In her grief, she was unable to engage with that world for the time being.

Once they arrived home, Sky crumpled onto the couch and stared at the ceiling with tears rolling down his cheeks. Kat sat beside him and put her arms around his shoulders.

She didn't try to say anything comforting; she knew nothing could ease his sorrow at present. Sitting silently on the couch together, Kat glanced at her laptop on a nearby table, unable to bring herself to open it. Whatever had happened over the weekend—in her business or in the world—simply did not matter. All that would have to wait.

When Sky had closed his eyes and curled up on the couch, appearing to be asleep, she quietly got up and went to her desk. Opening the front drawer, she pulled out some writing paper. She had not hand-written anything apart from her signature in years. But now, she felt repelled by her computer, unable to touch it. Instead, she felt compelled to write in longhand. Kat searched for a pencil and began to write a letter.

Dear Cancer,

You have so little courage. You hide in our bodies, and you don't appear until you have multiplied.
You are not prejudiced; you attack every race, religion, and sex.
You prey on every age. You have no shame. You are a coward.
Our family has fought you multiple times.
You attacked my little brother Max at age seven; he fought you multiple times into remission. At 11, you attacked him again. After giving him a bone marrow transplant, his body gave way, and he went on to heaven.

You made me believe that my marrow killed him. It controlled me for more than a decade. You are not only a killer, but you are a liar. I now know. I am forgiven, and you are sentenced. You have no conscience. You tried to make me weak, but you have made me stronger. We will someday defeat you forever.

You didn't stop with my brother. You hid in my father to later reveal yourself once again. He fought you valiantly. You tried to break his spirit, but you could not. He inspired many people and continues to do so through his legacy.

You have made your way into my friend's body. You refuse to quit, which makes you a tough opponent. You should know that I won't quit either, I AM RELENTLESS.

You may have taken the lives from our loved ones' physical bodies, but you cannot touch our spiritual bodies.

I forgive you, not for you, but for me, so that I may have peace while I continue to fight you.

Katerina Von Slyke

After finishing the letter to cancer, Kat read each line and repeated it in a whisper to really let each word sink in deeply. Cancer was an enemy that sought to destroy the security and happiness in both her and her son's lives. It was doing a damned good job at that! She reflected on what was really going on, why cancer was making so many appearances in her life right now. Could this hideous monster be a teacher? It certainly was bringing another situation in which she felt out of control. What was it that Vince always said about losing control, either internally or externally? She struggled to remember, her mind sodden and thick as sticky mud. Then it came to her: Vince said whenever you feel out of control, you are giving your power away. Then you've given your power to others, to the enemy.

Kat breathed out with a sigh, suddenly realizing that she'd been holding her breath. She had remembered her father's lesson about giving power away, and that was the first step. But, the next step wouldn't be as easy—she knew that she really needed to work on not giving her power away, and all she could do was let out another deep sigh.

TWENTY-FOUR

THE FOLLOWING TWO days were a blur to Kat as she numbly dealt with funeral and memorial service arrangements for her father. She somehow fielded interview requests from sports reporters and managed to consult with the local news obituary writer. It always struck her as strange that she seemed to forget how famous her dad was. The numerous condolences she received reinforced that reality. As they processed their grief, Kat and Sky spent hours reminiscing together about their wonderful memories of Vince. From time to time, they simply cried in each other's arms. Eventually, they would have to deal with Vince's house and possessions, but they put it off until after the funeral. They knew the task would be painful, and neither of them had the emotional capacity to take it on presently.

Thoughts about her usual routine crept into Kat's mind, but it seemed distant and unimportant. She had not gone for her early morning workout since her dad died, and had not even checked her laptop for messages related to work.

Finally, at 6 a.m. the next morning, when she still could not bring herself to go to the gym, Kat opened her laptop and turned on her cellphone. The laptop screen showed 324 emails, and her cellphone had 75 new messages. The only phone messages she had read the past two days were those about her dad.

She decided to tackle the emails first, since many would be work-related. She spent several hours responding to urgent communications from various members of her workforce. There were minor fires that she readily tended, and she appreciated her team's expressions of sympathy for her loss. Working her way backward, she was startled to find a disturbing email from her bank about the lenders. They were concerned that her investments had plummeted due to the plane that had been shot down. The bank warned that her lenders were threatening to recall their loans, since these were not now well-secured.

All the blood drained from Kat's face, and her hands started to shake. She owed 16 million dollars to the bank lenders, and if they did demand repayment, it could bankrupt her. Grinding her teeth, she swore under her breath about taking the risky step of over-leveraging her business to build the new store. It had been a gamble, and now the tables had been quickly turned against her. She checked the date of the bank's email to find it had arrived three days ago, silently wondering why there was no follow-up from them.

Heart pounding, she quickly turned to her cellphone and scanned the messages. There were eight missed calls in the past two days from her financial advisor, Tim. Now Kat's heart dropped like a lead weight, a sense of foreboding creeping over her. This could not be good. She didn't want to have a conversation with him where Sky might overhear, at least until she knew what was up. She quietly slipped outside the condo's front door into the hallway, noting that it was empty. Taking several deep breaths to center herself and slow her heartbeat, she called her advisor back.

Tim's voice was somber as he greeted her. First, he expressed condolences for her dad's passing and asked how she was holding up. He mentioned how much Vince's death had been featured on local media, which reminded her again of her dad's fame. Then he got down to business.

"So . . . I don't really know how to say this, but things don't look good," Tim said with slight hesitancy. "I don't know what your latest communication was with the bank, but, uh . . . it's serious trouble."

"The bank emailed me a few days ago that the investors were worried," Kat started. "Due to the stock market crisis maybe thinking my financial footing wasn't too secure."

"Uh-huh." Tim was silent for too long, and Kat's heart began pounding furiously again. "Kat, they've recalled the loan. The bank probably wanted me to tell you. They are giving you until the end of the month to make repayment."

"But that's impossible!" Kat cried. "This can't be happening; you know I can't make that repayment! Isn't there anything we can do? Some kind of renegotiation?"

"I'm afraid not. The loan officer was very firm. Of course, he expressed his sincere regrets, especially in light of your recent loss."

"We'll have to meet with him," Kat persisted. "Talk things over, get him to press the lenders for more time, or other terms—something!"

"Kat, you and I need to meet," Tim said in a firm voice. "I'll lay out all the figures in front of you and explain things. But I want you to hear this now: It appears the bank and the lenders will not change their demand. With your immense loan recalled, you don't have a lot of options. I've analyzed your assets, including your investments, and besides your business, you only have your property and possessions. The business is heavily leveraged. You knew that was a risk, and I advised against it. This is the unexpected complication that so often fouls up such unwise financial decisions. My preliminary conclusion is that you'll have to sell everything you have to pay off that loan. It's a fire sale, Kat. There's no other option that I can see."

Kat was stunned into silence. Only her gasping breaths let Tim know she was still on the phone. After a moment, he told her that he was really sorry and asked for a time when they could meet at his office. She muttered that she would call him back; she needed time to process this information. He warned that they had no time to spare and must meet no later than tomorrow. Kat agreed and punched off the call.

Back inside the condo, Kat sunk onto the couch next to Sky. Her pale, drawn face and tense body immediately alerted him to her distress. Kat's mind was in turmoil as her emotions lashed in several directions at once. How much more could she take? Anger vied with sorrow, fear pushed up against grief, while a gulf of hopelessness spread before her. She had lost everything. Her father, her brother, her friends, her marriage, her business, her home, her success . . . her life collapsed in front of her in shambles of ruin and destruction.

Sky got to his knees on the couch and wrapped both arms around his mom. He held her tightly and pressed his cheek against hers. Slowly her arms crept around him, and for a long time, they embraced silently. Neither could cry anymore; they had shed oceans of tears already. They simply fell into each other's hearts and offered wordless solace. After a while, Kat shifted, and Sky moved to sit beside her.

"I have to tell you something, Sky," Kat said in a low voice. "Everything in our life is about to change, in a really big way."

"It's changed already," Sky murmured. "Grand-dad is gone."

"I know. That *is* enough to change everything. But there's a more drastic change coming. The life we know, the life we've been leading, is about to go away. Completely." Kat looked directly into Sky's eyes as she continued.

"I'm about to lose the business. The bank lenders are demanding immediate repayment of a huge loan. I don't have enough money for that—unless we sell everything. We won't be able to live the way we have. I've totally failed in everything."

"Mom, it will be OK. I'm relieved that you're not sick, or something worse . . . what I really care about is that we're together. That we're OK and can stay together. As long as you don't have to go away, then I'm happy. We can adjust to living a different lifestyle. It's us continuing as a family that really matters. That's the truest success, Mom. Granddad would have said so. Remember how he talked about the 'Four Seasons to a Championship Life?' You're just moving into the next season of life . . . and being allowed an opportunity to grow from failure."

TWENTY-FIVE

"HEY, SKY, THROW me those cushions, will you?" Kat called across the front room of the Banff cabin. "There's still space in this box, and I'll fit them in."

Kat stood up to catch the pillows that Sky tossed in her direction. After shoving them into the large moving box, she groaned and pressed her fists into the small of her back. Looking around the cabin with sunlight streaming through windows, out toward the sparkling lake and trees with gracefully waving branches, sadness gripped her heart. She loved this cabin. It had been her refuge, a quiet place to slip away from work stresses and feel the peaceful embrace of nature. Now, she was spending the final few days there, packing things for moving out. She and Sky had taken on packing by themselves, trying to cut corners on expenses whenever possible. Vans from a local estate sale company were coming tomorrow to pick everything up. Hopefully, the estate sale would provide some much-needed funds.

Her financial advisor's worst-case scenario had come to pass. The bank lenders had recalled their loans, demanding payment by month's end. They had negotiated for more time, hoping that the new store's launch would bring revenue to offset loan repayments. But, when the new store in Montreal launched during the next month, its opening was a major flop. Revenue from her other stores could not make up the financial losses. By the end of the following month, Kat could not make payroll and had to start laying people off. Soon employees were leaving on their own, recognizing that the future of the business was bleak. Kat tried to find a buyer for Ace-It Athletics to keep the company going but got no realistic offers. It was a niche business and not appealing to many looking for easy markets.

Realizing she could not keep the company going, Kat closed all the stores and held a going out of business sale of clothing and accessories. Watching her business crumble was agonizing for Kat. She had poured countless hours, untold effort and several years of her life building it into a group of successful stores. Facing failure was foreign to her; she had been consistently successful until this point, relentless in pursuing her goals. She tried to remember her father's teachings about learning from failures, using them as lessons for evolving her growth. But, at the moment, her pain was too great to focus on anything else. Her mind felt numb, and she couldn't command it into action.

To pay off the huge loans, Kat had to put her condo in Toronto and the cabin in Banff up for sale. Even after using the inheritance she received from her father, she needed more money to meet these debts. Selling the cabin was the hardest thing by far and away. It held a special place in Kat's memories and her heart and was yet another significant loss. To her, losing the cabin was far worse than selling her private jet and the luxurious Mercedes Benz E550 AMG.

In the coming week, she and Sky would take a commercial flight from Calgary to return to Toronto and finish packing up the condo. After clearing out the condo, they planned to move into Vince's house, which he left to Kat. Mercifully, the mortgage had been paid off three years ago, and they could live there inexpensively while she figured out what to do next.

"Just one more room, Mom," Sky said cheerfully. "We'll be done by late afternoon and can take a sunset walk around the lake."

"Ummm," Kat responded listlessly, not knowing how to respond. Taking that walk as the sun cast golden streaks across the clear water toward the eastern mountains would be heart-wrenching.

"We can run into Banff for Thai food after that," Sky chirped. "That new Thai place is really good and pretty cheap. Our little Kia rental car gets great mileage, too."

Kat murmured again and nodded, eyes downcast. Sky came over and cupped her face in his hands, winking at her.

"Traveling light is going to be fun, Mom," he said. "Just think of it as new freedom from the responsibilities you've carried for so long. Now our burden is lighter!"

Kat gave Sky a defeated smile at his attempts to make things brighter, sighed, and followed him into the kitchen, the last room they needed to pack.

After returning to Toronto, they worked for several days packing things in the condo. Kat planned to hold another estate sale for the expensive furniture and decorative items. They agreed to keep only a few things that meant the most to each. Vince's house was fully furnished and really did not need much. Packing clothes and personal items was their primary focus.

Sky was concerned about his mom because he knew she was taking these losses hard. He had never cared a lot about the high-end lifestyle they led. Relationships and personal growth were always more important to him. Ever since he was little, Sky had learned life-shaping lessons from his grandfather, which were reinforced by his mother. But in the last few years, he watched Kat falling away from those lessons, finding it hard to apply them in her life. She seemed so out of balance, and too frequently, she lost control.

After lunch, Sky had a Saturday baseball game scheduled. Despite his fight with the bully Doug and temporary suspension from the team, Sky had been reinstated. Because of his dominating performance in pitching during tryouts, he was chosen for the select team. Today's game was one in a series against a neighbor school. Sky was deeply grateful that his slip-up in maintaining his center and losing control had not eliminated him, and he vowed never to "lose it" again in such situations. His grandfather's words echoed in his mind: "They can take your body, but they can't take your mind unless you give it to them." He would always remember that when in physically challenging encounters.

Sky's father was coming to take him to the baseball game. Kat wanted to keep working on packing the condo, since they were on a tight timeline to move out. Sky looked forward to spending time with his dad, especially now that they hadn't been able to get together recently. Glancing toward his mom, he had a sudden idea about how he could help her. He was worried she might be getting depressed and feeling hopeless. It was not good for her to keep going like this, falling into a dark hole.

"Mom, I'm going to my room for a little while," Sky said. "Be back soon. Need to get ready for Dad and the baseball game."

Kat nodded, pushing a strand of hair off her forehead. She turned back to sorting through books and dividing them between boxes to keep or give away.

TWENTY-SIX

THE CONDOMINIUM BUILDING'S front door signal rang, and Kat answered to buzz Bryce in. She had left her front door slightly open, and a few minutes later, Bryce came in, announcing his presence with a soft "Hi, I'm here."

Bryce glanced around, spotting Kat across the front room, kneeling beside the bookcase. He had never seen the place in such disarray. Boxes were strewn all around with wads of packing paper in disorderly heaps. Furniture had been pushed into two separate groupings, pictures removed from the walls and stacked against the furniture. Through the doorway into the kitchen, he could see drawers open, more boxes, dishes and cookware piled onto countertops. It was the expected chaos of moving.

Kat swiveled on her knees and looked up at Bryce. He was shocked at how terrible she appeared. There were dark circles under her eyes, and her face was pale and wan without any makeup. A green bandanna was tied around her forehead to hold back hair but was not doing a great job as tendrils escaped and fell across her cheeks. More telling, Kat's expression was weary, and her body seemed fragile as she slowly rose to her feet.

"Hi, Bryce," she said. "Thanks for taking Sky to his game this afternoon."

"Sure, I'm happy to do it," Bryce replied. He walked over to Kat and folded her into his arms, smiling warmly though his eyes were somber. "So sorry about everything," he murmured with lips pressed against her temple.

Kat leaned against Bryce, melting into his arms. It felt so good to have someone holding her, to feel the warmth of physical contact. She had long been missing affectionate touch from a man. She was jarred by the deep ache inside that reminded her how much she missed this. Memories of their good times together flooded into her awareness, unbidden and bittersweet. Would she ever resolve the loss of their marriage? She could feel the love that still remained between them, despite their conflicted separation.

Bryce broke their embrace after what seemed an inappropriately long time to him. Yet he wanted to keep holding Kat, comforting her and giving her strength.

"How're you doing? You're not looking so good, are you alright?" Bryce said.

"Good as I can be, I guess," she answered. "Yeah, I'm not looking my best."

"Moving is always such a bear. One of my least favorite things, along with just about everyone else. Looks as if you're making progress, though."

"Uh-huh. We're slowly getting there. I'm sorting through stuff, deciding what to sell and what to keep."

"I saw the estate sale advertised online," Bryce commented. "Hope you get good prices, lots of your furniture and decorative items are really valuable."

"Thanks, yeah . . . my taste has been pretty upscale, but all that's changed," Kat said with a wry laugh.

"Your dad's house is comfortable, if not chic," Bryce said. "Sky will fit well there. Speaking of, where is he?" Bryce looked toward the door to Sky's room and yelled: "Hey Sky, are you ready? We need to leave pretty soon."

"Be there in a second," came Sky's muffled answer through the closed door.

Bryce placed an arm around Kat's shoulder and gave her a gentle squeeze.

"I'm a little concerned about leaving you alone now," he said. "You look so stressed out. Are you sure you'll be OK alone here this afternoon?"

"I'll be OK. I really do look worse than I feel," Kat tried to reassure him. "I just need a little time to process things, to cope with all the changes."

"You wouldn't do anything crazy, would you? You know, people get desperate and depressed . . . do something they might regret."

"No, really. . . I'm not falling apart that much." Kat tried to put conviction into her voice and looked up at Bryce with as big a smile as she could muster.

Sky's door flung open, and he ran out dressed in full baseball gear, his bag slung over his shoulder.

"Ready to go, Dad," Sky said cheerily. He went to Kat and embraced her with his free arm.

"Good luck in the game," Kat told him. "Demolish those batters as you always do."

"Thanks, Mom. Oh, could you take a look inside my room? I'm close to finished packing, but don't know what to do about the furniture. Could you help me decide what to keep? Like you're making different groups of things out here, which to keep and which to sell."

"Sure, I'll take a look," Kat responded with a smile.

Bryce and Sky left, and Kat was alone in the condo. The silence settled heavily onto her, and she plopped down on the nearest chair. Propped against it was one of her favorite pictures, an Impressionist painting of a springtime garden in France. It was worth a lot of money. She was torn whether to keep or sell it. This thought threw her into grief about everything that had departed and was in the process of leaving her life. Unbidden, tears rolled down her cheeks as a surge of despair flooded her emotions.

It would be nice just to have things end, simply to stop all this sorrow. Not to feel anything for a while—or ever again.

She was grateful for Bryce's concerns over her mental health. He was right about her abject state of mind; it was as low as she could ever recall. But she wasn't a quitter. She had learned from her father about "fighting the enemy" wherever it showed up. Vince had told her that nothing is neutral, that you're always either getting closer to your goal or farther away. The enemy could be opinions of others, fear, laziness, or your own interior dialogue. He said to rate every decision on a scale from "intelligent to stupid." That would give sure guidance whether it was a good decision or not.

She knew any decision to harm herself or decompensate would be on the stupid end of the scale. It would move her farther away from the goal of recovering from her losses. It would be terrible for Sky, and she could not do such a thing to him. She would fight this enemy.

Shaking her head, Kat tried to clear her mind and settle her emotions. With a grimace, she thought that having a few more coping tools at hand would be helpful. If only she could remember everything else her dad had taught over the years.

Kat stood and walked into Sky's room to find out how she could help with his request. As she entered the room, she saw that the shelves, dresser, and closet had been emptied out, books and clothes placed in boxes. Several pieces of furniture were pushed against the walls. In the middle of the room was one large wooden box, its lid closed. She went over to the box to see what was inside.

TWENTY-SEVEN

THE WOODEN BOX in the center of Sky's room was well-crafted and painted with warm-toned varnish. There was a brass plaque on the lid with Sky's name engraved. Kat could not recall ever having seen this box before. She knelt down beside the box and ran her hands over its smooth surfaces, filled with curiosity. Carefully unlatching the brass hinges in front, she slowly opened the lid. On top of the box contents was a neatly folded piece of paper with Sky's handwriting.

"Hi, Mom, I hope this reminds you."

Kat was puzzled about this cryptic note from Sky. Since it was clearly addressed to her, she assumed this meant that she should go through the box contents. She felt a little reluctant to rifle through Sky's papers, but it appeared this was what he wanted. The box was filled nearly to capacity with notebooks and loose pages. These must represent years of collecting and storing things important to Sky.

After opening a few notebooks and glancing at some papers, Kat realized they held his personal journal entries and reflection notes. Again, she felt hesitant to go snooping through Sky's writings, but he obviously wanted her to do just that. Maybe she should start with journals closer to the bottom of the box, assuming these were written at earlier dates. She found one journal from three years ago. Sky was writing about the physics exam he had failed that year, and how badly he felt about it. He examined the reasons why his test performance was so bad, finding cause within himself for not studying more or seeking tutoring. The page was crumpled as though he had meant to tear it out, but later smoothed it down and kept it in his journal. The last entry on that page said, "Look for the lessons."

When she turned the page over, she saw he had written: "Nothing is neutral. Everything you do is either taking you closer to or farther away from the goal. You can learn from every experience, no matter how painful. You can make a more intelligent decision the next time. Grand-dad's model for successful decision-making."

The next journal was from last year. One section caught Kat's eye, where Sky was writing about an encounter with a girl at school. He wrote about how pretty and sweet she was. It had the undertones of a first infatuation, and Kat blushed at reading her son's yearnings. Quickly she closed this journal and put it away. This seemed too personal, and she didn't feel right about continuing to snoop. Best to let her son retain certain secrets.

A recent journal dated the current year came into her hands next. Sky was writing about his tryouts for the special team in baseball, going through his goals and plans for achieving them. Then she saw his comments about the encounter with Doug during the last tryout game. Sky did a masterful job of analyzing his reactions and how he was giving away his power to anger and reactivity. He admitted how pissed he was about losing his temper and letting himself get into a fight with Doug. He reviewed lessons from Vince about the model for keeping your power intact, even in difficult situations. He quoted Vince, saying, "They can take your body, but they can't take your mind unless you give it to them." He enumerated the steps he could have taken to remain in control and not give his power away, using Vince's LSGT model (Learn, Study, Grow, Train).

Next, the journal addressed Kat's outbursts in the principal's office and later in the car driving home. He had been embarrassed by her attempts to place the entire blame on Doug and the umpire, and again acknowledged the role he played in the incident. Sky observed that his mom had been on edge lately, not acting as usual and losing her cool too much. He reminded himself to be patient with her, to keep calm, and be as supportive as he could while she tried to work things out.

Another entry a week later talked about how distant his mom had been for some weeks. Apparently, her obsession with work had hit an all-time high, and he surmised she must have been facing significant problems. Sky expressed his sadness that their time together was not as loving and fun as it used to be. He regretted that they didn't seem as close as before, and wanted desperately to bridge that gap. The next entry described how angry his mom often was, with such a short fuse. Sky again reminded himself that she was under a lot of stress; to be patient with her, to make things as easy as possible. He did not want to become reactive himself and add more fuel to the fire.

After these entries, Sky recorded a brainstorming session he went through to come up with ideas to help Kat's company, including the Tik-Tok influencer plan. It was obvious that he had put a lot of work into this session. Kat was deeply touched by his demonstration of caring, and she felt her emotions beginning to break down.

She was now seeing herself from another person's perspective. It caused her remorse to learn how much Sky had altered his behavior to support her and help her recover her balance—becoming aware of Sky's own struggles during this time simply added to her guilt. Instead of being sensitive to his situation and giving him support, she had been totally immersed in her own needs and troubles. She never wanted to cause Sky hardship, but that was precisely what she had done. What kind of a mother was she? Sky was far more caring and mature than she had been, as if their roles had reversed. The time for her to provide him with support and comfort in his recent challenges had come and gone.

Kat sat back on her heels and returned Sky's latest journal to the box. She got quiet inside and took a few deep breaths. There were powerful lessons here. She knew she could do better; vowed that she *would* do better. Reflecting on her son's notes, she realized she had plenty of recent opportunities to be the observer of her responses to situations and make good choices about taking action. However, she had not maintained enough self-awareness to keep on top of reactions and provide space for better decisions.

Again, she read the note Sky had left in the box for her. "I hope this reminds you." It most certainly did remind her of her father's years of guidance. Now, she determined to re-activate these teachings in her life.

TWENTY-EIGHT

KAT RETURNED SKY'S journals to the box and settled his note on top, where he had left it. Closing the lid, she glanced around his room and noticed that the furniture he had placed near the walls made two natural groupings. It was not hard to figure out which group he wanted to keep and which to sell or give away. She chuckled to herself at the ruse he employed to get her inside his room, where she would see the conspicuous box.

Returning to the kitchen, she shoved aside some plates, found a glass, and filled it with water. After a deep drink, she set down the glass and walked over to the large window looking out over the high-rise condo's well-manicured gardens and fountain. Beyond that, the cityscape of Toronto stretched into the distance. These were reminders of all she had lost recently—her business, her exclusive condo, the cabin in Banff, the Mercedes and the private jet. Most of her wealth had just evaporated. Only her inheritance from her father kept her from being destitute and provided a place for her and Sky to live.

Thinking about the inheritance painfully brought Vince to mind. Once again, the intensity of grief over his death assaulted her emotions. She felt sincere regret that she hadn't spent more time with him during his last month of life. It pained her to recall how she tried to blow him off when he wanted to meet and tell her about his cancer. Then how she promised to accompany him to chemotherapy but backed out, using work pressure as the excuse. There were no excuses for her behavior. She had been selfish and uncaring, absorbed in her problems, and thus missed out on precious time with her dad.

A litany of her less-than-admirable behavior in the past few months ran through her mind. She thought of how her son was affected by her anger and preoccupation that put distance between them. How her reactivity had created scenes with waiters and embarrassed her friends, how the fight in the mall parking lot caused trouble for Vic and derailed an important discussion, how snippy she had been with the condo valet. She even regretted how critical and unappreciative she had been with her employees.

Pacing in front of the window, Kat felt as if she were entering a trance. She felt her usual state of awareness slipping away, as if she were floating like a disembodied observer above her head. Now this observer could see Kat's actions from an entirely different perspective, and the view was a disturbing one. How could she have been so blind to her own actions? So oblivious to how these affected other people?

This Kat, the selfish and unobserving one, was not who she had been raised to be. The true Kat was above that, a finer person, and could do better. Reading her son's journals had reminded her, and she had vowed to course-correct using what she had learned from her dad. It was time. She must do it now.

She returned to perching on the kitchen stool and took more sips of water. As she drank, her mind rolled around the numerous models that Vince had taught her over the years. There were so many that she was at a loss where to begin. Suddenly, an idea popped into her mind—a beginning place that Vince said always gave you a good start. He repeatedly said, "Make a list of what you're grateful for."

She eyed a notebook a few feet away that she had left for making lists of items for the estate sale and smiled slightly. Still perched on the stool, she grabbed a pen, opened the notebook, flipped to a blank page, and wrote on top "Things I Am Grateful For."

The first entry was being grateful that her son had reminded her to be the observer of her own life. She had fallen away from this essential practice for too long. The journals in his box not only gave insight into his viewpoints and experiences but put her in touch with her own behaviors. She felt driven to write about these recent events, to express her feelings in this concrete way in a journal, just like her son and dad had done.

The pen flew over the pages as Kat poured her heart into expressing feelings about all her acts of commission and omission: the angry, out-of-control, combative ones and the blind, oblivious, self-centered ones. She wrote about her failed company, the poor decisions that led to that, how she often was not present for others, how her temper created trouble, her lack of awareness with friends and family. Episode after episode were relayed on the journal pages in an immense internal release, a cleansing.

She began to see the patterns as she expressed herself in the journal. All of a sudden, it became clear how all these events proceeded from thoughts, to emotions, to words, and into actions. She remembered that Vince emphasized how all success starts from the inside—what he had called the "Inner Game"—how everything that first began on the inside then moved to the outside. The Inner Game also includes energy movement through the mind, body, emotions, and spirit. You had to begin on the inside; to make changes there first. "All success and failure," he had said, "starts from the inside."

Gratefulness was a good way for her to reconnect to the Inner Game. As she meditated on a few things she was thankful for, an image of her father burst into her mind as clearly as if he were in a video on her cellphone screen. He was standing in the middle of the empty Blue Jays stadium when she was about 10 years old. She sat in the infield watching him wind up on the pitcher's mound, throwing across the plate to an imaginary batter. It was one of the many times they went to the empty stadium together, where he explained the fine points of baseball and the success principles he followed.

"Most important, Kat, is the Inner Game," he had said. "The key to success in this Inner Game is focus. See, Kit-Kat, I feel grateful for being on the Blue Jays team, for wearing this uniform. I'm grateful to be playing this game, and never want to take it for granted. Every game I play, I give my best, but when it's over, I leave that performance on the playing field. Any mistakes or errors stay right on the field. I leave with no regrets, only gratitude for playing."

"How is gratitude connected to the Inner Game?" she had asked.

"It's a part of the Inner Game and balances energies. When you're working this Inside-Out Process, you need to have mind, heart, body, and soul in alignment. To get the level of focus that puts you 'Into the Zone' requires right thinking, leading to right feelings and behaviors, and creates the habits leading to peak performance. Having gratitude for playing keeps you away from negativity, which could reduce your ability to focus."

"So, it's all about using the Inner Game for focus?" she persisted, striving to understand.

"When you're on the mound, you need total focus," Vince explained. "You need to block everything else out, to narrow your focus to just pitching. That puts you 'Into the Zone' where you can reach peak performance. Being in the Zone is what gives the edge. You don't want anything to interfere with getting Into the Zone."

"So, if you worried about past performances, that could interfere with the Zone," she had offered. "And gratitude plays a part?"

"Gratitude helps to put us in the right mindset, but it's not *all* about gratefulness. Gratitude just helps put us in the Zone. It all begins with how you're thinking. The state of your thoughts," Vince said as he picked up a ball.

"Consider this: When you are focused on the task at hand with no distractions, just like I've been doing from pitch to pitch, that's what makes the difference between success and failure."

Vince wound up and threw another pitch, which sped perfectly over the plate in the strike zone. He turned to her and smiled.

"Think about it, Kit-Kat—it's hard to be anxious, scared, or upset when you are feeling grateful."

Kat thought for a minute and then said, "I guess that's so."

"And that allows you to focus completely on what you're doing. For me, it's throwing the next perfect pitch."

TWENTY-NINE

"WHAT I AM Grateful For."

Kat stared at this title for some moments as a flood of emotions cascaded through her, along with numerous memories. *Begin at the beginning,* she thought.

"My parents. I am grateful for both of my parents." She remembered her mother's softness and the scent of violets she often wore. Comfort and love were freely given by this kind-hearted woman who left Kat's life all too soon. She admitted that she harbored some resentment toward her mother for dying early, even as her mind told her that compassion was the right emotion. *OK,* she thought, *I admit the resentment and am sorry about it, even though I was only a child. It's understandable to feel that way.* Kat wrote all of this in the journal.

Her father had played such a huge role in her life that she hardly knew where to begin. He was a solid, dependable presence who brought strength to everyone in the family.

He was an outstanding example, and she was privileged to have learned all the success principles he lived out so well. When the family consisted of just the two of them, he was her constant companion and closest friend. Almost every success habit she used in her life came from him. Now she felt undeserving of this great role model. In the past few years, she had fallen away from the principles and techniques she had learned from him.

That was no way to honor his memory, she reflected. *OK, Dad, I can do better—and I will from now on.*

She wrote these realizations in the journal and expressed her unending gratitude to her father. As a reminder for future reference, she made a list of as many of her dad's lessons as she could bring to mind. She planned to revisit each one to refresh her understanding, to identify how it applied to her life now, and to grow in the ability to carry it out.

She ended the list with the model that got her started. A surge of love and profound appreciation for her father welled inside Kat's heart. She realized he would always be beside her, as long as she remembered him and thought often about him. He was still her inspiring teacher and constant companion.

Expressing gratitude for the next family member was easy. After reading Sky's journals, she realized just how much he cared for her and the immense efforts he made to be supportive. She was also struck by how wise her son was, far beyond his years. He was consistently applying the models she and Vince taught him, using them for learning and growing into a finer person. She was delighted that Sky was following in her footsteps, the same path that she had taken with her father. Kat felt chagrined to admit that her son had internalized Vince's lessons far better than she had. Sky had now become her teacher, getting her back on the right track. She wrote sincere expressions of gratitude for Sky as her heart filled with love for him.

There was one other family member, her brother Max. As she thought about him, her pen hovered over the page. Did she really want to go there? Did she want to revisit that terribly painful place in her life? After some consideration, she decided that she did want to resolve her brother's death, something that was long overdue.

Kat allowed memories of her brother's valiant fight against leukemia to flow through her mind. She revisited the fear, worry, confusion, and uncertainty during his series of chemotherapy treatments. She felt the pain of watching Max suffer bravely, unable to do anything to relieve it. Then there was the short time when he went into remission, and she recalled how happy the family had been. But the enemy came crashing back in, and Max was in desperate circumstances, unable to receive more chemo. Bone marrow transplant was the only hope, and among the family, her marrow was the best match. Eagerly she agreed and submitted to the painful marrow extraction, praying for a good outcome. Things seemed to be going great, and Max was to be discharged when his condition quickly deteriorated. His body had rejected her bone marrow and was shutting down. Within a short time, Max died.

The weeks of grief that followed were a dark pall to Kat, but she permitted all the despair and guilt to surge up. She had blamed herself for causing Max's death; her bone marrow had literally killed her brother. She was angry at God and the world for letting her brother die at such a young age. But even more, she was furious with herself for the role her bone marrow played in his death. This anger had never really left her.

With tears in her eyes, Kat wrote the words she had never been able to say.

"I forgive you." She intended to forgive Max for leaving too soon and causing the family such a burden of grief. But she realized that she was actually forgiving herself. This was key, and Kat knew she must make it very clear. With trembling hand, she wrote the words that she had buried inside for decades:

"I forgive you, Kat, for the death of Max." Next, she added, "Kat, you did everything you could to help, and that is enough."

As she finished writing this sentence, she felt an immense weight lifting from her heart. Her chest felt lighter and she drew in a deep breath, filling her lungs as if she had been underwater for too long. She could breathe freely again. She hadn't noticed before just how tight her chest felt.

But she had more to say to Max. She needed to find ways to be grateful for the experience.

"I am grateful to you, Max," she continued writing. "You taught me the hardest lesson of all—acceptance. I learned there are things beyond my control. Your cancer was not something I could control. You do your best to make things better. After making your top effort, really putting all you've got into it, and things don't improve or work out . . . that's when you need to let go trying to control the uncontrollable. That's when it's time for acceptance."

She reflected for a few minutes, seeing links with other teachings of Vince. He said to ask yourself if you would do it again, and if the answer was "Yes," then to let it go. If the answer was "No," then it was up to you to change; to honor the defeat or setback.

Kat knew the time to change was now. She had to stop beating herself up.

"Honor what you tried to do. Not to change means that I am dragging the anchor along with me. Do what it takes and honor the times you have been late to do so and see that you are changing. Appreciate your suffering as a teacher. Then you can change and be hopeful about the future." Vince's words reverberated deep within her heart. He had not won every game he pitched, but he knew he needed to let that go, forgive himself, and move forward.

"I guess acceptance is part of the Inner Game," she wrote. "That's when struggling to control things is not the smart choice. Just let it go."

Vince said you could learn to appreciate your suffering. One of his favorite Bible verses taught: ". . . we rejoice in our sufferings, knowing that suffering produces endurance, and endurance produces character, and character produces hope . . ." (Rom 5:3-4 ESV) You can appreciate suffering as a teacher who strengthens and spurs growth. It makes you hopeful about your future; motivates you to keep following your dreams and goals. In the end, it makes you able to handle more success.

"Max, you were my teacher for enduring and appreciating suffering," she wrote. "I couldn't see it for a long time, but you've also helped me become capable of true success—a whole and balanced life. Max, you truly taught me how to live."

Kat began crying softly as she put down the pen. But this time, these were tears of joy and release. She could have sworn that she felt Max smiling down on her at that moment. Internally, she again expressed gratitude to her brother.

Thank you, Max, for helping me release this burden of guilt. I am grateful for the time we had together, little brother. Be at peace. I love you.

After crying for some time, Kat became quiet and peaceful inside. Soon a growling stomach alerted her that it was nearly dinner time, and she was hungry. Bryce would bring Sky home soon. She went to the fridge and pulled out a frozen pizza, noticing that it was their favorite type for movie night. She smiled and turned on the oven.

THIRTY

AS THE PIZZA cooked, Kat continued writing a list of things she was grateful for in the journal. She scribbled rapidly as one thing after another flew through her mind. Her life had definitely had its ups and downs, but through it all, she could see the numerous blessings. She remembered inspiring teachers, great childhood friends, wonderful vacations, and the many competent and dedicated co-workers and staff of her business.

Bryce, her ex-husband, came to mind, and she cringed a little. Memories of their good times together made her wistful. So much about their marriage had been good. He was honorable through their divorce and remained supportive after they were living separately. And, he was a wonderful father to Sky. She felt remorse for treating him with such hostility and realized she had acted like a jerk.

Realizing her hand had begun cramping from writing nonstop, she put down the pen and shook her hand in attempt to bring it back to life. As she took a break, she mentally thanked her father for teaching her this exercise of expressing gratitude. He had told her to do it whenever she was having a bad day, but truth be told, she hadn't done it in years.

Yes, Dad, I am definitely going to do better remembering your lessons, she thought.

The oven timer beeped to announce that the pizza was done. She glanced at the journal and realized she had written at least 50 things she was grateful for. Smiling to herself, Kat turned off the oven and took out the pizza. Her timing turned out to be perfect—Sky and Bryce opened the door to the smell of melted cheese and pepperoni.

She picked up the pen and quickly wrote two more things in her gratitude list:

"Bryce. Frozen pizza with Sky."

Kat greeted them and asked how the game went. It was another stellar performance by Sky whose pitching was again domineering, and his team won handily. Bryce gave several examples of key plays and complimented his son, which brought forth a big smile from Sky.

"Bryce, will you stay for pizza?" Kat asked.

"Thanks so much for the offer, but I can't stay tonight. Evelyn cooked dinner and is expecting me," Bryce replied.

"OK, maybe another time," said Kat. "I'll walk you out while Sky washes up."

Sky dashed off to his room as they walked toward the door. Hovering at the doorway, Kat looked up into Bryce's eyes. As ever, she was struck by how handsome and kind his face was.

"Bryce, I, uh . . . I wanted to thank you for being such a good father to Sky."

He appeared a bit surprised but smiled and nodded.

"It's so nice of you to say so," Bryce said. "Sky is really easy to get along with; he's an exceptional kid. I'm just happy to be able to see him so often, stay involved in his life."

"Uh-huh." There were implications in those comments that Kat needed more time to process. She knew too many situations where divorced parents remained embattled, and the ones who suffered the most were the kids. Although she had never tried to put up barriers to Bryce's seeing Sky, she had avoided getting closer to his new family. Her attitude toward Evelyn was hostile, and she tried to avoid interacting with Grace, their daughter. As if it had just dawned on her in the moment, Kat felt a flush of shame for this mean behavior.

Bryce was turning to go when Kat reached out and touched his arm.

"Um . . . Bryce? There's something else I want to say," she murmured.

He turned back to face her, eyebrows raised in curiosity.

"About us; about our marriage," she continued. "I'm sorry about our marriage falling apart. I realize a lot of it was my fault."

Bryce's face registered surprise, his eyes widened.

"It's hard for me to say this, but I really want to," Kat rushed on. If she didn't push through now, she knew she might not be able to say it in the future. "I was wholly self-focused for many years. I made my business success the ultimate priority and drove myself relentlessly to attain my goals—at any cost. Now I see how that pursuit pushed you to the edges of my life. I didn't make time for our relationship, ignored your needs, kept expecting you to 'get with the program' and go along with my ambitions."

Somewhere along the line, Kat forgot an important principle her father had taught her: whatever you don't feed dies. "You get from life what you give to it," Vince had said. "Whatever you don't give to, you get nothing in return. Simple as that." Looking back, she knew her marriage failed because she didn't feed it.

"When our marriage was in trouble, I wouldn't compromise. I was too driven to pull back, to meet you halfway."

"Kat. . ." Bryce began.

"No, let me finish. Bryce, I'm so sorry. After you left, I felt like a failure. I wanted to belittle you, to put down your abilities to cover up my mistakes. My anger was out of control, so I lashed out and treated your new family abysmally. There's no excuse for my rude behavior, even the overwhelming pain I felt inside. Anger and pain, they're not really a winning combination. Now, those two have led to my losing almost everything. But this disaster has taught me something truly important: that money isn't the only important thing. It's really shown me the value of family, of relationships."

Tears were trickling down her cheeks, but she smiled at him hopefully.

"I've learned that it's OK to have different opinions. I respect your choices, and don't see your goals as inferior to mine. I hope you'll accept my apology."

Bryce took a hesitant step toward Kat and placed a hand on her shoulder.

"I do accept it, Kat. Thank you for saying this to me," he said softly. "I'm also very sorry that things didn't work out. We had a lot of good times, didn't we?" His voice was wistful.

Kat nodded and looked down. She put her hand over his that rested on her shoulder.

Bryce closed the distance between them and gathered Kat in his arms, hugging her tightly. She relaxed into his embrace and placed her cheek against his chest.

"Kat, I'll always love you," Bryce whispered. "Even though our lives are now separate, and the love has to be expressed differently, it's still there. Always has been, even through the worst times."

A mixture of sadness and happiness filled Kat's heart. She felt grief over the loss of their marriage, which she'd never before allowed herself to admit, covering it up with anger. She felt gratitude for Bryce's constant caring, both for her and Sky. She felt the peace of acceptance settle over her.

"Bryce, I'll always love you, too," she said softly, face pressed to his chest. "We can share our love through our son. I'm OK with it now; I can accept things as they are. I want you to be happy with your new family."

"Thanks, Kat." Bryce kissed her forehead, then released her and held her at arms' length. "I hope you'll take another chance on love. You've got a lot of life ahead of you, and you're a wonderful person. You'll find a good man and have a happy relationship."

Kat smiled and nodded. They waved goodbye, and Bryce went to take the elevator down.

THIRTY-ONE

AS THEY SHARED their favorite pizza, Kat and Sky talked about his box, the journals that she read, and her list of things she was grateful for. She laughed at his obvious ploy to remind her of her dad's lessons for living a successful life. He teased his mom gently about forgetting to use these great models and principles that were their legacy from Vince. They studied her list of lessons from Vince, and Sky asked which one she wanted to focus on. After thinking, Kat said she really wanted to plunge into understanding "The 8 Forms of Wealth." This lesson seemed vitally important now as she began to re-frame her approach to success.

Kat turned to a fresh page in her journal, and they brainstormed together as she took notes. Sky reminded his mother that first, she needed to rate or grade each area of wealth on a scale of 0 to 10, with 0 being terrible and 10 being excellent.

"Hold on a sec, lemme go grab something!" Sky said, jumping up to go to his room. Grabbing a journal he knew well, he came back and opened it up to go over the assessment instructions with his mom.

"So, the rating is supposed to be how you feel about each area right now; your assessment of how fulfilled each of these is for you. Then you explain why you gave it that rating. It's an honest look at all these aspects of life, and how well you believe you're doing.

"Then, you describe what a 10 looks like for each area. This gives a picture of your life vision for each area of wealth. It's based on what your vision is today; what your belief level is today. Naturally, your vision could change as you learn, grow, and experience more. The vision of a 10 in each area of wealth provides a goal that you desire to achieve. It sets your direction and motivates you toward success. The vision is how you imagine fulfillment would look and feel. Sound good?"

He passed the journal over to Kat, telling her to read through the 8 Forms and write down her ratings, one at a time. She smiled, again expressing gratitude internally for her son, who was wise beyond his years.

The 8 Forms of Wealth

"Developing this vision is all about fulfillment. You can also think of it as the 'Wheel or Circle of Life' since it encompasses

all the important areas of a complete and balanced life. If one area is not doing well, then it's hard to be truly fulfilled."

1. **Family:** Family provides the foundation for our lives. Having and maintaining loving and supportive family relationships is one of the greatest forms of wealth. Families that affirm our worth offer a sound foundation. If families fill us with self-doubt, we may struggle with self-worth, but there are ways to deal with negative thinking. Our beliefs, values, and goals are shaped by family; though other influences enter our lives, that family core stays with us. As Tony Robbins says, "We live who we believe we are." Other forms of wealth may come and go in our lives. We can lose our money or careers, but if we have a loving family surrounding us, we are still wealthy in the most significant way.

Kat rated herself a 5 in Family. Her losses, failed marriage, and hostility toward Bryce's family were sources of suffering. Now she was in the process of improving these, creating a more loving family for Sky. Her vision was a healed, congenial, and supportive family, however it might be structured.

2. **Relationships**: Many types of relationships are formed during our lives: personal, social, business, professional, mutual interests, hobbies, and others. Some are short-term, and others last a lifetime. These

enrich our lives and must be treated with respect and honesty. They keep us connected to a larger swath of living. If we don't give energy and attention to relationships, if we are not present, then the quality suffers.

Kat rated herself 6 in Relationships. She had formed successful business and professional relationships, although she was aware that her difficulties in delegating and acknowledging had diminished the quality. Her lack of being fully present for friends such as Vic reduced her ability to provide support in times of need. She was making amends with Vic and several co-workers from her former business, but her long-term vision was to have open, attentive, mutually supportive, and enjoyable relationships with others.

3. **Finance**: Financial success involves earning and creating monetary resources that are enough to support your desired lifestyle. Ambitious people might seek higher levels of financial success that bring extreme wealth and world-class lifestyle. The measure of financial success has more to do with a lifestyle in which your needs and desires are satisfied than your assets and income.

Kat rated herself 5 in Finances. She had attained a good measure of wealth and upper-level lifestyle during the heyday of her sporting goods stores. Although she had lost that, and dropped considerably in financial standing, she was not destitute—thanks to her father. She was moving into another phase of life and felt optimistic about creating a new financial future. Her vision was to rebuild sound financial standing and be more prudent about using her assets. The dream of a wildly successful financial future hovered in her awareness.

4. **Career**: Having a successful career is a path for self-expression and realizing your abilities. It provides opportunities for creativity, commitment, dedication, stamina, and rising to become the best in your field. By constantly building toward Peak Performance, you can expand your career success to nearly unimagined heights. Pursuing a career is character building, offering challenges, and demanding that you overcome obstacles. Setbacks and failures serve as a lesson to advance you toward the next level of success.

Kat rated herself 6 in Career. Her interests were in sports-related business, and she had created a chain of highly profitable sports clothing and accessories. She had dedicated immense effort and attention to her career, but it was to the detriment of her family and relationships. Bad financial decisions led to losing her company. She saw how interrelated these areas of wealth were, and was now working on how and why the business failed. Her vision was a career that was both successful and self-fulfilling, and also compatible with success in the areas of family and relationships.

5. **Health and Fitness**: Keeping the body and mind healthy and fit are important values for a satisfying life. Regardless of financial or career success, if you are in poor health, it is hard to enjoy them. Part of the discipline necessary for success can be built through an active lifestyle with regular exercise and healthy nutrition.

Kat rated herself 9 in Health and Fitness. She had developed a demanding exercise regimen years ago and stuck to it, keeping her body trim and strong. For the most part, her diet was healthy, except her propensity for pizza with Sky. A little break from health-nut nutrition was also a sign of flexibility and not being fanatical. Her vision for this area was to continue her practices, seeking a balance with other areas of wealth.

6. **Lifestyle**: Having a successful lifestyle depends on identifying your goals for how you want to live and making plans to achieve them. This could be following better health practices, having more social activities, being involved in charitable causes, community activism, religious community, professional organizations, and many others. Where you live, the type of housing and neighborhood, are important

aspects of lifestyle. Making conscious choices about these involvements and your home is critical in reaching your goals.

Kat rated herself 7 in Lifestyle. She had aspired to a world-class lifestyle with exclusive condominium, cabin in Banff, private jet, and expensive car and had attained those. In her career, she participated in organizations and causes, following a clear purpose for advancement. Now, her lifestyle was changing dramatically, scaling down and moving her into different circles. This was a transition she would learn from, developing endurance and strength to rebuild toward her next lifestyle choices. Her vision was a lifestyle that met both her needs and those of her son, Sky. It was not yet clear what that would be.

7. **Personal Development**: Learning is the foundation for successful personal growth. Personal development involves learning and getting mastery of your mind and emotions. You approach all life's experiences as teachers. Whatever career path you choose, mastery of yourself is essential to become the best in your field as possible. This learning and mastery aid your growth in finding ways of self-expression that are compatible with your values and goals. When you are well-rounded and balanced in life, then you are developing to your highest potential.

Kat rated herself 5 in Personal Development. She realized the importance of a personal growth plan that would help her succeed in all areas of life. She had been narrowly focused on success in business and finances, neglecting other areas of life due to her driving ambition to expand her business. Now she was taking into account what other aspects of personal development needed attention. Her vision was to learn and grow in all areas of life by mastering her mind and emotions.

8. **Spirituality**: This aspect of wealth can be very different for people. It's not all about religion or faith, although for some it can be. Spirituality is about your soul, about what enriches your soul, which is the indwelling spirit and essence of a person. Many believe that your soul is the part of you that makes you who you are, and that will live on after your death. It is the spirit in animate life, and spirit connects you to the Infinite Being. For many, spirituality is experienced through nature, which provides both inspiration and cleansing.

Kat rated herself 3 in Spirituality. She did not follow any religion, but did find spiritual experiences in the natural world, especially forests, lakes, and mountains. However, she had neglected this aspect of wealth for too long. Her soul felt impoverished and in need of healing. The cabin in Banff had been her source of spiritual replenishment, but even that was eroded by her obsession with business success. Her vision was to regularly spend more time in nature, to consciously feel its cleansing power, and to take inside the enrichment it provided.

THIRTY-TWO

SEVERAL MONTHS LATER, Kat and Sky had settled into Vince's home after completing the sale of the high-rise condo and estate sale. They now lived in a distinctly different neighborhood, with homes widely spaced on large lots, near a park with walking paths and children's playground.

Sky actually liked this suburban lifestyle more than the mid-city high-rise condo. It felt relaxed and friendly, with more young people and opportunities to meet and mingle. He didn't miss the valet service and chauffeur driving him to school, the security protocols for entering the condo, or the breath-taking view from the higher floors. Now he took a bus to a new school, and that was fine with him. He had finished the year at his former school and played out the baseball season, leading his team to the regional championship.

Kat was having more trouble adjusting. Her prior "world-class" lifestyle was a goal that she had struggled mightily to attain. Scaling back so much was humbling, and she was still dealing with lessons that it brought. Her financial situation was concerning—she had not sought employment, as working for someone else was too hard after running her own business for years and calling the shots. While crunching the figures to see how long she could stay off work, she felt encouraged that her stock market investments were regaining value. Her mind danced with entrepreneurial ideas. She was following her father's models every day, choosing which one to work with as things came up. Some days, however, she decided to select one of her father's teachings and focus on it. Today she was grappling with the concept of "Being Present."

From examining the mistakes she'd made in the past several years, it was clear that one of the biggest was not being present with others in the moment. Sure, she had definitely been adept at "Getting into the Zone" with business activities. She had whole-heartedly pursued her goal for business success. All distractions were pushed aside and ignored so she could give every ounce of mental, physical, emotional, and intellectual energy to the tasks at hand. She maintained 100% focus and, in turn, it brought financial success. But removing distractions that would diminish effectiveness had too often included other people. She had not been present for family or friends, which had destroyed her marriage and caused anguish to friends such as Vic.

Kat realized that Getting into the Zone was an out-standing state of being when you needed to accomplish something during a specific time. Her dad had used it frequently during his baseball career, and so did Sky. It gave them the laser focus needed to pitch a dominating game. But she now saw that this kind of focus had its proper time and place. She had kept it up to the detriment of the principle of being present.

Wisdom, she thought, *must be the ability to discern and make intelligent choices about which principles to use.*

To accomplish that, she realized she needed to become the constant observer of her thoughts, feelings, and actions in every moment. It was a tall order, but it would lead to the next level of success. "To become the observer," her dad had told her, you needed to have your heart and mind in perfect alignment. "You must be present in the exact moment, be aware of feelings, and watch yourself instead of simply reacting. Where your mental and emotional state come together *before* you react," he said.

But what if your heart and mind were battling? How can you stay present and be the observer when you're angry? Vince advised documenting every feeling you have when you get angry or upset. Write them down, notice the sequence in which feelings happened, and describe what was going on in the situation. Once you can see the chain of events, you can understand your triggers and find ways to defuse them. You can examine the discrepancies between your thoughts and feelings, bring the disconnect to light, and identify your true intentions. Then you can reprogram your responses and bring both the heart and mind into alignment.

She remembered one of Vince's pithy remarks that encapsulated this principle: "Never walk into your house with dirty feet." What he meant was, don't bring anger and worries into your home life; leave your anger at the doorstep. Get your heart and mind into alignment for the sake of your family so you can be truly present with them.

Kat heaved a big sigh. She felt her heart and mind battling right at that moment, trying to reconcile these principles and just getting frustrated. *What was that other piece of advice Dad had given?* She thought, chuckling as she remembered: "When your heart and mind are battling, take a walk."

Grabbing a light sweater, Kat headed out the door to take that walk. At first, she strode vigorously to stop her mind from spinning. Soon she had to take deep breaths to maintain the effort, and she felt her mind emptying out. She looked up at the sound of birds chirping and spotted a flock of sparrows in the treetops. Slowing down, she listened to their soothing chirps and soon noticed the lush, green grass and flowering shrubs lining the path in the park. She veered into the park and was simply in the moment, enjoying nature. For her, nature was cleansing and spiritual. Her heart felt light, and her mind was calm. She observed what a pleasant, expanded state it was.

Suddenly her calm was interrupted by a dog bounding across the grass. Tongue lolling and ears pricked forward, the beautiful gray and white Siberian husky came straight to Kat and leapt against her legs. His piercing blue eyes seemed to call to her.

"Well, hello, gorgeous," Kat crooned, rubbing behind his ears. "Where did you come from?"

The husky, pleased at her attention, danced around her, wagging his tail.

"Max! Max! Come back!" a baritone voice called.

Kat looked up and saw a man running across the grass in the direction the dog had come from. A leash was dangling from his hand. When he reached her, he quickly grabbed the dog's collar and reattached the leash.

"I'm so sorry," he said breathlessly. "The clasp slipped, I don't know how. I hope he didn't hurt you."

"Oh, no, not at all!" Kat smiled at the disheveled but quite good-looking man, his brown hair tousled and hazel eyes showing sincere concern.

"Good, good. Usually I'm careful to make sure I put on the leash since he loves to run free. It's his Siberian husky nature, you know." He smiled ruefully at her, creating two charming dimples in his cheeks.

"Huskies are great dogs," Kat replied. "Have you had him long?"

"Only two years, but he's the captain of my heart," said the man. "My only heart-throb at the moment. I haven't seen you before, are you new to the neighborhood?"

"Yes, my son and I moved in about six months ago. We live just up that block," she pointed behind her. "I'm Kat Von Slyke, nice to meet you."

"Von Slyke? You must be related to Vince Von Slyke. Are you living in his house?"

"Yes, I'm his daughter. How did you know?"

"It's not a common name, and Vince is famous in these parts. I know where he lived and that he passed away last year. I'm so sorry for your loss." He paused and offered his hand. "Very pleased to meet you. My name is Frank Gireaud. I've followed your father's career for years; I'm a sports agent. Pitchers don't come any better than Vince. He was a remarkable manager, too."

"Frank Gireaud, yes! I've heard your name. You represented a few of my dad's teammates, as I recall," Kat commented.

"Well, it's a small world, so they say," Frank retorted with a big smile. "Welcome to the neighborhood. I feel as if we're already friends with a lot in common."

"I'll bet you've done lots of negotiating, dealing with professional athletes and managers," Kat said. "I could probably learn a thing or two from you."

Frank laughed and said, "Yeah, it's all about being present; tuning into meanings behind words, listening with both heart and mind."

"Those are just the skills I need right now." Kat wondered at the synchronicity of life, bringing a wise teacher into her path. She recalled how Vince talked about stacking meaning, how giving more meaning to something gives it greater importance, which brings better focus.

"Yeah, focus in the moment is key to being present," Kat continued thoughtfully. "My dad always told me that."

The dog had been sitting obediently at Frank's feet but seemed to need to run a bit more. It sprang to its feet and pulled hard on the leash, jerking Frank's arm sharply. He laughed and said, "Whoa, Max, take it easy. OK, we'll continue the walk. Kat, would you like to come along with us for a bit?"

Kat startled as she caught the dog's name. Although Frank had called him by name before, somehow it had escaped her notice. *Dang!* she thought. *I'm being unobservant again.*

She joined Frank and Max as they set off along the path at a smart pace. After a few minutes, she decided to ask about the dog's name.

"Your dog is named Max? How did you choose that name?"

"Some kind of intuition," Frank replied. "We French Canadians are quite sensitive, you know, tuned into things. I had this dream one night of a very brave boy named Max. Huskies are brave, loyal, and caring. He seemed to share these qualities with the boy, so I chose the name for him. Why do you ask?"

Kat gulped before she could reply.

"My little brother, who died of cancer, was named Max."

THIRTY-THREE

KAT RANG THE doorbell at the front entrance to Bryce's house. She waited with a little trepidation for someone to answer. Usually, when she picked Sky up after a weekend with his father, she sat in her car and texted him to come out. Now she was changing things up, creating new patterns, and wanted to reach out to Bryce and his family.

Bryce appeared surprised when he opened the door. He welcomed Kat and invited her inside, walking beside her into the family room where everyone was gathered playing a board game. They all looked up with puzzlement on their faces.

"Uh, I'll grab my things, Mom," said Sky. "Is everything OK?"

"Stay for a moment, Sky," she replied. "There's no problem; I just wanted to say 'Hi' to everyone."

"Well, sure, have a seat," said Evelyn. "Can I get you something to drink? Tea, coffee or something stronger?"

"Coffee's fine, if it's no problem," Kat responded.

Evelyn went into the kitchen and Bryce sat on the couch next to Kat.

"How're things going? You're looking really great," he said.

"Pretty good, all things considered," Kat answered. "We're getting used to living in Dad's neighborhood. It's nice to have sidewalks and parks with paths, lots of greenery around."

"I liked it from the very beginning," Sky offered. "There's a diamond in the park, and I've been playing some pick-up baseball with other guys who live nearby. Of course, I don't throw quite as ruthlessly as in real games. I let them get some hits, makes it more fun."

Bryce and Kat laughed, causing little Grace to look up from her game and join in.

"You're practicing the fine points of making friends," said Bryce.

"I've made a friend, too," said Kat. "Would you believe that the sports agent, Frank Gireaud, lives in the neighborhood? You remember him; he represented some of the players on Dad's team when he was still playing."

"Yeah, I think I do recall him," said Bryce. He detected a faint blush on Kat's cheeks. "Nice guy, huh?"

Kat nodded, her blush deepening.

"We're going on a date next week," she murmured.

"Well, I've got to meet him soon!" Sky exclaimed.

Evelyn came in with coffee for the adults and juice for the kids. Conversation switched to the kids' activities, and Bryce shared proudly about how well Grace was doing in pre-school. Sky talked about his new high school and how much he liked his science and literature teachers. He had easily made it onto the baseball team and was developing friendships with the other guys. Kat appeared genuinely interested in everyone's comments, even when Grace tried to describe her favorite games with friends.

Evelyn was watching the interactions closely, thoroughly surprised at how pleasant Kat was acting. This was the first time Kat had ever been polite and friendly to her and the family. She was curious about the marked change in Kat; it appeared to be a 180-degree shift. She'd make a point to ask Bryce what he knew later.

Kat had, in fact, been studying her dad's "180-Degree Mindset" principle. The lesson was to observe your thoughts, assess the state of your thinking. This was especially important when these thoughts were creating tension and distress. She understood that thoughts led to emotions and actions. "Fix your thoughts," Vince said, "and then reactions and actions will follow. It's all about replacing a negative thought with a positive thought." If she could determine to hold the opposite thought, then behaviors would follow, leading to relaxation and comfort.

She knew that her interactions with Bryce's family had been edgy for years, if not outright hostile. Determined to change this, she examined the underlying thoughts and feelings that pushed her to behave badly. Eventually, she admitted these were residuals of her anger and resentment toward Bryce for leaving, divorcing her, and starting a new family. Intermixed was jealousy at the happiness he found and a selfish desire to diminish it by being hurtful to his wife and daughter.

At first, Kat berated herself harshly and felt ashamed of her unpleasant behavior. Eventually, she worked toward accepting that it came from her inner pain, all intertwined with the death of her brother and the guilt she felt over it. She had forgiven Max's leaving too soon, she had forgiven Bryce, and now she had forgiven herself. This gave her the inner peace to change her way of thinking, so she could also change her feelings and behaviors toward Evelyn and Grace.

Kat turned toward Evelyn and engaged in conversation about her interests and activities. Evelyn had worked as a librarian but quit to be a full-time mother for Grace. She continued involvement with the book world by attending several book clubs and doing volunteer activities for the local library. They asked each other about favorite authors and were soon sharing enthusiasm about recent books they had read.

As that conversation concluded, Evelyn glanced toward Bryce and placed a hand on her abdomen. He nodded almost imperceptibly, but they were so attuned that she knew his meaning at once.

"Um. . . there's something we'd like to tell you, Kat," Evelyn said. "We're expecting another child. The doctor just confirmed that it's a boy, due in six months."

"I'm gonna have a little brother!" Grace chirped. "Then I'll have a big brother *and* a little brother."

"That's right," said Sky. "Surrounded by brothers, what a lucky girl."

Kat felt her stomach clench. She knew she had to immediately become the observer to be able to choose her response instead of going with her gut reaction. Kat understood quickly that her reaction was due to sadness because she and Bryce never had more children together. She acknowledged her regret and then simply let it go. She chose to be enthusiastic and supportive of Evelyn and Bryce. That was the best thing for Sky, too. The mindset to always take the high road, treat others with respect, and be kind was what her father had taught.

Becoming the observer allowed Kat to control her state of being. It brought the ability to create clarity and awareness, giving a deep understanding of herself and the situations she found herself in. In this state of heightened awareness of thoughts and feelings, she could choose the best reactions.

"Oh, Evelyn, that's so wonderful!" Kat said. "Congratulations to you and Bryce. And to you, Grace, you'll have so much fun with both of your brothers."

Grace clapped her hands and giggled, tossing her golden curls. For the first time, Kat noticed how cute Bryce's daughter was and felt a surge of love for the child.

"Come here, sweetheart," she said, opening her arms to Grace. "Let me give you a big hug and be happy along with you."

Grace went over to Kat and hugged her.

"Are you my auntie?" Grace asked.

"Yeah, kinda," said Kat, laughing. "I'd love to be your auntie."

And at that moment, all the tension left the room. Conversation flowed easily, and the love between them was nearly palpable. Bryce and Evelyn exchanged glances, still a bit shocked but entirely happy over the change in Kat. After a while, Kat said she and Sky should be getting home, as it was near dinnertime. Evelyn offered that they might stay for dinner, but Kat didn't want to impose on such short notice.

"Let's plan for dinner together soon," Kat said. "Sky and I would love to begin doing things together with you, sort of like an extended family."

"Yes, we can go to Blue Jays games together!" Sky added enthusiastically. "And movies, and to the mall shopping, and ice skating, and picnics and all those things."

Everyone laughed, stood up, and embraced all around.

"We'll certainly do a lot of things together," said Bryce as he walked Kat and Sky to the door. He smiled at Kat as she left, whispering, "Thanks, champ."

THIRTY-FOUR

THERE WAS MORE that Kat believed she could learn from the failure of her business, Ace-It Athletics. In recent months she had made significant changes in her personal and family relationships, working on her Inner Game and aligning her heart and mind. Now, she and Sky got together with Bryce's family every two weeks. They enjoyed doing a variety of things, getting more at ease with each other. Kat could see how Sky and Grace blossomed in this loving, supportive family atmosphere.

When Frank had come to pick up Kat for their date, she introduced him to Sky. The two made an immediate connection and were immersed in baseball conversation within a few minutes. It was remarkable how much they both knew about baseball history, trivia, and the trajectory of Vince's career. They agreed to go together to an upcoming Blue Jays game. Later, Sky confided in his mother that he really liked Frank. She had his full approval to continue dating this fine man.

Kat decided to take an in-depth look at what worked and what didn't work in her business, reflecting on her past performances. She had identified key elements, and was now keeping a journal on her computer. She documented the bad habits that crept into her routine over the years, and noted ideas about how these derailed the success of her business. She knew that nothing was neutral. Each action followed a choice and either moved her toward or away from the goal.

There were three things in particular that she found problematic: underlying anger leading to loss of control; failure to give acknowledgement and appreciation to her employees; and over-leveraging her business. To further analyze these and make changes, she applied her father's LSGT principle.

Each element received a separate application of the LSGT model:

ANGER

L – Kat had already learned about her anger and done considerable work on it. She realized that it came from the pain and loss she experienced as a youth and became a defense mechanism against being hurt again. It did fuel her drive for relentless success and seemed effective for a while, but eventually backfired. By losing control repeatedly, Kat alienated people and created difficulties. It cost her marriage and nearly cost her friendship with Vic.

S – Now, by studying it, she understood the anger process and its triggers. By staying observant of her feelings and thoughts, she could catch the flare-up of anger at its onset and make a choice. She realized that choice for another action was always possible. She did not have to be reactive.

G – To grow from these insights, she would apply techniques that made possible a better choice for action. When she felt rising anger, she could immediately breathe to calm her mind and emotions. This bought her time to consider what the best action would be. She could change what she was feeling on the inside from anger to observation, stay present in the moment, and become centered. When she felt calm and present, she could then choose a more intelligent and effective response.

T – New behaviors needed to be solidified by repetition. This was the training part of the model, a resetting of neural pathways to make these her default responses. Kat had been practicing this reset for many months and felt it was becoming a habit.

ACKNOWLEDGE AND APPRECIATE

L – During the exercise of writing what she was grateful for, Kat had learned how many people contributed to her life and success. In relation to her business, she remembered so many loyal employees who had worked hard and were keys to the business' growth. Sadly, she had not given them the acknowledgement they deserved. They no doubt felt unappreciated.

S – She studied a few incidents in detail to fully grasp the significance. The incident of the "blue-bird" athletic influencer came to mind. Even though the skating star Cayla Cateau had specifically mentioned her employee Nancy was the key to garnering endorsement, Kat just ignored it and never thanked her employee. Imagining how she would feel if treated that way filled Kat with compassion for Nancy. In another instance, Kat rarely showed appreciation for her personal assistant Sara, taking this consistently loyal and devoted employee for granted. How long would talented people such as Nancy and Sara continue working for an unappreciative boss? This was a major failing of hers, Kat admitted.

G – Kat believed she had already grown from these realizations. She recognized that her poor leadership was a key factor leading to deficiencies in team performance. Had her leadership been stronger, employees would not have started bailing when the business was in financial trouble. In addition, if she'd been more caring toward her workers, they might have hung with it longer.

T – Never again would she overlook being appreciative of co-workers and colleagues. This required awareness, being the observer, so she would not miss those opportunities where a word of praise was particularly meaningful. Part of her work routine from now on would be making a commitment to watch for things to appreciate and acknowledge.

OVER-LEVERAGING

L – This was the most painful lesson of her business failure. She learned that listening to her advisors and taking careful stock of risk-benefit ratios was vitally important. When unexpected international events impacted her financial status, the huge loan she had taken out to open the new store in Montreal was called back. There was always potential for such complications, and she should have considered how it would affect her precarious financial balance. She couldn't repay the loan without selling everything and closing her stores.

S – Kat studied why she made the risky decision to over-leverage her business. Her own business sense made her apprehensive about the huge leveraging, but she was driven to attain ever-greater success. *Pride and ambition before common sense*, she reflected. She had been over-confident in her abilities to handle the situation. This clouded her judgment.

G – Growing from what she learned was absolutely essential for future business ventures. By losing everything, she gained a perspective of what life is like at rock bottom. It made her understand the roller-coaster ride of being a peak performer. When you play big, live world-class, and become over-confident, you can lose big. Kat resolved to never again leverage her success in ways that could lead to losing it all.

T – She took the attitude that losing big was part of training for the next level of success. Her experiences had spurred a re-examination of what success meant. It broadened her definitions of success to include all aspects of her life, not just business and career. As she practiced living in this new perspective, she entrained those values.

Kat looked up from her journaling and realized she had been typing for hours. Her fingers ached, and her stomach growled. Still, she felt enlivened and empowered from the insight and growth work she had done.

Going to the fridge, Kat searched around for something quick and found a carton of leftover poke. It was perfect for eating cold. Taking it out, she grabbed a beer and sat at the table, munching away and feeling gratitude for the quick meal. While she did enjoy the poke, she thought it could be better. Maybe the sauce could be more original, the combination of veggies and condiments more creative. Poke was really popular now, especially among the healthy lifestyle and athletic groups, but the local options were limited.

An idea sparked in her mind. She could certainly create better poke. Why not start a new business, a poke franchise? Poke was among the healthiest foods and an outstanding immune system builder. It was made with high-grade tuna full of omega-3 fatty acids and quality protein, and fresh, raw vegetables with numerous antioxidants, vitamins, and minerals. Creative sauces added sparkling flavors and raised poke dishes to gourmet levels.

She knew the demographic that loved good poke. It was the same one that her former sports clothing and accessories business attracted. She could create an innovative approach to franchising that drew in families of entrepreneurs and infused high-performance coaching to ensure their success. The more Kat thought about it, the more excited she became. Her business model would create a remarkable culture and set a new standard.

In her vision, she saw these poke franchises spreading across the world. This was her next path to peak performance success—and she would involve many others, engaging them to live lives without limits and realize their dreams and goals.

THIRTY-FIVE

SKY, FRANK, BRYCE, and Vic sat with anticipation around a small conference table in Kat's modest office that she rented in the neighborhood business center. They were invited to be the first audience for her new poke franchise business model. She valued their feedback and wanted to learn from their assessments. From the beginning of this journey, Kat held the intention that her next career venture would involve both families and co-workers in a joint creative endeavor.

Kat had prepared the presentation following her father's 9 Point System for Success in Life. The model included all aspects of life, drawing from the 8 Forms of Wealth model. Aware that her former approach to success had been too heavily weighted toward career and finances, she first worked the system for herself, creating a vision for each area: Family, Relationships, Finance, Career, Health and Fitness, Lifestyle, Personal Development, and Spirituality. Some of those areas were still works in progress for her, but she felt good about where she was headed.

The presentation today focused on Career and Business. It would be the under-girding for her poke restaurant franchise business. In Kat's approach, she incorporated the lessons she learned from mistakes in her previous business. In her mind, this was a "success after failure" model—a path to bounce back and realize a broader vision of her dreams and goals. As she talked to the small group, Kat displayed slides from her PowerPoint presentation on the TV monitor attached to the wall.

"This is my vision of the life I want to live over the next three to five years," Kat said. "I've written this vision as though I am already living my dream life. I'm going to create an innovative and highly successful poke restaurant franchise. I'm setting goals for my career and business; a franchise that will include families of entrepreneurs, first in Canada and the United States, and eventually across the globe. The magic ingredient is high-performance coaching to ensure solid business practices at each step, to support people in reaching their individual peak performance, and to encourage continuous personal development. As my dad would say, they will be able to live a championship life."

She went through a series of slides that described the model, step by step:

Step 1 – Setting Goals:

List your top 10 goals for Career/Business. Hold a clear vision of these goals and create a mental picture of the desired outcome. Believe your dreams are possible and imagine what success looks and feels like. Write down these goals to solidify them. From among these, select the top 3-5 goals that you believe will truly help you achieve your vision. Then, pick one goal that, when achieved, would have the most significant impact on your life. This is your Impact/Focus Goal.

Step 2 – Behaviors:

Starting with your Impact/Focus Goal, list 3-5 behaviors that will best help you achieve this goal. Determine what habits are needed to attain the goal. New behaviors turn into habits that create new skills. Start small with achievable behaviors, since fast results reinforce motivation. This lays the foundation for large changes that lead to success. Be sure you have the fundamentals of new behaviors right since bad techniques will not bring superior results. The key is consistency. Make these behaviors daily "musts" and measure results.

Step 3 – The Why:

Your reasons for accomplishing goals are the jet fuel for action. These must be big enough to carry you through tough times. Your personal "Why" is the cause that lives deep in your soul; the reasons come first, and the answers come second. This is personal and powerful, and nothing can take it away. "Why" must be clear, unshakeable, and deeply meaningful, so nothing causes you to lose sight of goals. This is what pushes you beyond obstacles and keeps you fighting.

Step 4 – Sacrifice:

Every new accomplishment comes with sacrifice, small or large. List a few things that you can give up in the short term so you can have a championship life in the long term. Big goals take time, and you need to avoid instant gratification. Bigger goals require bigger sacrifices. You must be willing to overcome adversity and realize that the pain of discipline weighs ounces, while the pain of regret weighs tons. Reaching peak performance is just the beginning of higher-level success, and staying at the top of your game takes as much dedication and hard work as getting to your goals.

Step 5 – Fighting the Enemy:

Along the way to high-level achievement, you will encounter obstacles that try to sabotage success. An enemy is anything standing in opposition to your goals. It can be current or past circumstances, others' opinions, discouragement, health issues, injuries, lack of belief, self-doubt. Make a list of a few enemies. When you identify and become aware of enemies, you begin to conquer them. Learn to protect your vision and remember that *only you* can keep yourself from accomplishing goals. Many times, the further you feel from a goal or dream, the closer you are to a breakthrough. You must realize that your dreams are worth fighting for and learn to disempower what opposes your success.

Step 6 – Decision Time:

You have the power of decision over your life. Decisions shape your life, and if you don't make them, you are just accepting what life brings you. Make a committed decision that you are going all-in toward goals; this cuts off the possibility of failure. Tony Robbins said that the three decisions shaping your life are as follows: what to focus on each moment, what this means, and what you should do now. Take a decision-making pledge affirming you are willing to do whatever it takes to achieve your goals. You will learn from setbacks, but these will not derail you.

Step 7 – Working Partners:

Every successful person, organization, or team has working partners. These are coaches, mentors, and partners who shorten the learning curve to peak performance and greatness. Make a list of people who are currently helping you to achieve greatness (coaches, mentors, partners). If you do not have them or need additional ones, list people you can reach out to.

Step 8 – Take the Quit Option off the Table:

When things get hard, do not consider quitting. If it were easy, everyone would be living a championship life. Realize you are worth the struggle. When you feel tired and beat up, go back and review your vision statement. Reclaim the excitement you had when you started. Keep moving forward and make needed changes in behaviors, routines, and sacrifices. Identify new enemies and reaffirm your decision to go all in. Call in your coach or mentor and take an action step now.

Step 9 – Game Plan:

You need to plan your work and work your plan. You cannot manage this process if you don't measure it. Use daily, weekly, monthly, quarterly, and annual measurement systems to keep you on track to reaching your goals. For each Impact Goal, list the behaviors needed to achieve it. Evaluate how you are carrying out these behaviors, listing what you need more of and less of. State your "Why" for this goal, and list actions that will best achieve it in the areas of sacrifices, enemies, decisions, working partners. Note what you need more or less of.

One of the systems for measurement is applying the Sunday Game Sheet. The Sunday Game Sheet allows you to both look back and look forward to prioritize within your Game Plan. For example, on Sunday evening (or another evening that fits your lifestyle), you take time for reflection, maybe 15 to 30 minutes. You make a weekly recap, writing down the following four things: what you need to do more, what you need to do less, what you learned that week, and what you're grateful for. Then, set priorities for what you need to accomplish.

"To illustrate this 9-Point System, I'll work through the steps using my first Impact/Focus goal," Kat said. "My vision is to create an entrepreneurial franchise of fast casual poke restaurants with creative fusion dishes that become the standard to which other companies set their benchmark. The initial Impact/Focus goal is to establish the flagship restaurant in Toronto and make a profit by the end of the first year."

She advanced a slide with these two statements. For each of the next eight points, she showed an accompanying slide and narrated.

"The most important new behaviors for me are collaboration and delegation with my start-up team. As you know, these have not always been my strong suits," Kat smiled ruefully. "Vic is on board as co-owner of the franchise, and we are establishing a cooperative, mutually respectful relationship. Each member added to the team will have a voice in how the business operates, and their contributions will receive regular acknowledgement. Even the smallest person in the room will feel valuable. Everyone will know it's a team effort from the start.

"The 'Why' for me is to honor my brother Max by showing I'll never give up, and by creating a business model he would be proud of. He faced extreme challenges without complaining and kept fighting. This business is for us both. He is the inspiration that always fuels my efforts.

"I'm willing to sacrifice other activities that I enjoy during the start-up phase. I'll devote immense energy and put forth extreme effort, keeping up the discipline of following this system."

Kat paused and looked at each person present, then said resolutely: "I won't let my dedication ruin my relationships. I am confident I can do this and maintain balance in life.

"Fighting enemies is something I've done all along. The biggest enemies now are my past habit of over-focusing on work to the detriment of other parts of life, and the inability to delegate. I intend to follow a harmonious work pattern, learn to delegate, trust others, and create truly collaborative success.

"The decisions immediately before me are recruiting talent to make the poke restaurant a reality—a creative chef, imaginative builder, marketing experts, experienced cooks and wait-staff, and wise financial advisors. I've learned that people are the difference-makers in any endeavor. Whether you win or lose always comes down to the people on your team. When you've got the best team you can find, you must be willing to delegate, to let them use their abilities. This was an important lesson for me; I won't get the best results by trying to control everything.

"Vic and I are already in this process. With Vic's invest-ment capital and the rising value of my stock market hold-ings, we're starting on sound financial footing. We've taken a pledge to let nothing stand in the way of our world-class poke restaurant. And, we'll never over-leverage.

"My main coach is my father, Vince. By studying and applying his models and principles, I've got nearly all the guidance I need. I'm depending on my son to keep remind-ing me about them," Kat winked at Sky, who smiled back broadly.

"Though now I'm in the excitement of putting my vision into motion, I realize I'll get discouraged at times. For me, there is no option to quit. I know I'm worth the effort to keep going until we've got the most popular poke franchise in the world.

"The Game Plan will guide efforts as we go forward. I've set up a measurement grid that will track the attainment of daily, weekly, monthly, quarterly, and annual goals. Examining how this is proceeding will give me pointers to where changes are needed."

Kat brought up the final slide of her presentation. It showed a globe with glowing red dots in most continents. Across the top, the name of her business flashed:

"Peak Performance Poke."

THIRTY-SIX

THE ALARM WOKE Kat at 5:30 a.m. She swung out of bed, dressed, and grabbed a power shake before heading off to the gym. She had now been following the new routine for three years, and she deeply appreciated getting another hour of sleep in the morning. After working out for an hour, she returned home, took a shower, and spent 30 minutes either studying Vince's lessons or writing in her journal. Then she dressed to go to work at 8 a.m., spending a few minutes catching up on Sky's plans for the day.

On the way to her new poke restaurant, she stopped at a coffee shop to meet her business partner, Vic. Her best friend had successfully completed breast cancer treatments and was in remission. When Kat was creating the poke restaurant franchise, she had discussed ideas with Vic, who wanted to pursue a new career direction. Vic brought investment capital to help get the start-up business going, and they formed a partnership.

Sky was going to the local community college for his first two years. After taking foundation courses and thinking over career options, he would select a major and apply to the university. Being in college gave Sky a more flexible schedule, and he even had a car now! Sky was working part-time at his mom's restaurant to help out and earn pocket money. He continued involvement in baseball, playing for the college team, and was still considering a major league career in the footsteps of his grandfather.

Kat considered her present routine a new expression of The Championship Hour that had guided her prior business success. She well knew the importance of that first hour of your day. The patterns built during this key time would shape behaviors for the rest of the day, and ultimately, for life. Healthy eating, regular conditioning and strength-building exercise, reflection, and a positive attitude were essential for a satisfying and effective day. Upon repeating such days, your success in all aspects of life would be enhanced. In keeping with her goal of more balance in life, she liked the modifications of her routine that allowed more rest and study in her schedule. She felt sure her dad would approve.

It was a big help for her to apply Vince's model of The Four Seasons of a Championship Life as she recovered from business failure and built a new career. Identifying the season you are in helps you structure what your zone will look like, and where you need to focus. First comes pre-season, the training time when you're developing new skills and techniques, building upon basics, and establishing new habits. You invest time and energy into improvements, building partnerships, and laying a sound foundation.

Next comes the in-season, "game time" when you channel the skills you've built into the "game"—in her case, the business. This is the zone of total focus, correcting any weaknesses and honing your abilities. You work closely with your team, with roles and relationships already established, as you grow together and fine-tune your efforts. Then you reach the post-season where you've attained success. Most people don't get to the post-season; it's like making the championship series in baseball. You trust each team member to fulfill their role. Trust is the key element, and all team members are relentless in striving for peak performance. Habits are now automatic, and the team knows it has what it takes to reach the top. Being in the zone means everyone focuses on doing individual tasks with precision and excellence. It's the culmination of the prior two seasons, and you reward yourself for progress.

After that comes the off-season. This is a time to rest, reflect, relax, and rejuvenate. Everyone needs time to have fun, take vacations, and live without stress. Without taking breaks from work, people will burn out. During the off-season, you look back and evaluate your performance over the past year. This reflection helps you get a better perspective on future directions. It supports the goal of maintaining peak performance for as long as possible.

Life is full of change and challenge, Kat had learned. Things can happen that are beyond your control, and you must learn to adapt and grow from difficulties. Kat had seen the entire process in her sports clothing and accessories business—training to success to failure to reflection, and then to recovery by bringing a new business to the world. In the process, she had learned and grown significantly and expanded her ideas of the successful life.

Vic was already perched at a tall table when Kat arrived at the coffee shop. They waved, and Kat went to the counter to order a latte. Waiting for the barista to make the latte, she noticed that he looked familiar. When he brought the perfect creation with a leafy swirl on top, she remembered him. It was Felipe, the valet who used to work at her high-rise condo. He smiled as he gave her the latte, and she felt a flash of embarrassment recalling how she had responded nastily when he inquired how she and Sky were doing.

"Hello, Kat, how's it going?" Felipe asked.

"Hello, Felipe! Things are good," Kat answered. "Do you like your job here?"

"Sure do, it's an outlet for my creativity," he said with a laugh. "I'm going to chef school, and this is a start."

Kat noted that his appearance had changed a good deal. He wore his hair shaved on the sides with a long tendril behind and had a small gold earring in one ear.

"That's a nice-looking earring you're wearing," she said. Taking the latte, she admired its design and remarked,

"You're a skilled barista; this is beautiful latte art. Nice work. You'll make a great chef."

Felipe smiled and was obviously pleased with the compliments.

"Thanks for noticing," Felipe said. "Hope you have a good day and enjoy yourself."

"Yeah, thanks, and same to you."

"I will," he remarked. "I learned a few things from you about having a good day. . . you know, in that valet job at your condo."

"Gosh, I'm so sorry I was rude to you at times," Kat said sheepishly. "I've learned a few things about good days and a good life since then."

"No doubt we've both grown from our experiences. We always have choices, and it seems you've made a few good ones; you're looking really relaxed and cheerful. You were always pretty tense before."

"That's so true!" Kat felt an impulse to reach out toward Felipe. "Come by my new poke restaurant sometime; I'll treat you to lunch. It's just down the block."

Felipe smiled and nodded, saying he would love to try her restaurant. Kat smiled at him and felt genuinely happy at their pleasant reconnection. She observed how much better this felt than their previous interactions. *By embracing yourself as the observer*, she thought, *you really can become a better person.*

Kat joined Vic at the tall table, and they chatted about things at work for a while. The new restaurant was growing in popularity and getting good culinary reviews in local media. They had a congenial staff and made certain to always recognize the workers' contributions. Projections looked excellent for the store to be profitable by year's end. Plans were being drawn up for the next few franchises, and finances were falling nicely into place. Both women focused on teamwork and principles of success, having staff trainings in which Kat taught many of Vince's models and techniques. Again, Kat felt deep gratitude for everything her father had given her, and she continued to draw from his spirit. He would always be an inspiration and guiding light.

"How are things with you and Frank?" Vic asked after a lull in business talk. "You've been a steady item for nearly four years."

"It's all good," Kat replied. "We're edging closer to making the commitment. But, we don't want to rush into things."

"You won't be accused of that!" said Vic.

Kat laughed and reflected on how much better relationships were going now in her life. Treating others kindly and taking their needs and viewpoints into consideration had made a world of difference. But, she couldn't have done that without rediscovering her father's lessons and going through a major self-assessment. Vince would certainly be happy about how effective using these lessons were in changing her Inner Game, learning the importance of Being Present, using the Power of Gratitude, and applying the LSGT model.

Now, she was again in the pre-season of the Four Seasons of a Championship Life, building skills, partnerships, and a sound foundation for the poke restaurant franchise. Her confidence soared as she thought of the power that the 9-Point System brought to her team, and the principles of teamwork she had learned. She was eager to move the business into the next season, where all the skills, abilities, and focus of her team would achieve increasing numbers of entrepreneur families joining with their own franchises.

A vision of the post-season, with franchises operating successfully around the world, flashed before her. It was a vision that included many people, many families, many cities, and many countries. A vision of mutual, shared success in a business that promoted healthy lifestyles. It filled her heart with happiness and gratitude.

THIRTY-SEVEN

APPLAUSE BROKE OUT all around the conference table as Kat walked into the room. She smiled and nodded to her managers seated around the table. Vic entered the room just behind Kat, and everyone at the table rose to their feet, applauding both women enthusiastically. After expressing appreciation for their recognition, Kat asked all to be seated and began the meeting.

It was the fifth anniversary of the founding of Peak Performance Poke, and the home office managers were assembled to receive the annual report. The head of operations gave the overview of their global expansion; they had 1,100 poke franchise restaurants in 10 countries in North America, Europe, Asia, and the Pacific Islands, with another 300 in process.

The chief of marketing used a slick PowerPoint presentation to demonstrate how they found such an effective formula for capturing the world's imagination about the potential of poke. He emphasized how they struck just the right demographic, speaking eloquently to a wide age range of people who valued an athletic and health-promoting lifestyle. Their double whammy was offering delicious, uniquely flavored poke that was also an immune system builder.

The next report was by the managing chef, who oversaw menu planning and introduction of new flavor profiles. Kat felt especially gratified when Felipe stood to give his presentation. After her former valet finished culinary school, she had hired him for the menu team. Before long, Felipe's talent for creating unusual Pacific Islands flavorings led to these dishes becoming top favorites in the poke franchises. His ability to work well with a variety of people and implement programs effectively led to promotion within ranks. His talent as a manager gradually unfolded, and soon, he was on the home office managing team.

The head of finances reported that the overall financial picture of the franchise company was excellent. Nearly all the franchised restaurants were operating in the black, and most were making a handy profit. When restaurants needed help, an operations team was sent to mentor and coach them. The operations team composition depended upon where the store needed work to succeed; it might include the head chef, best trainer, or top financial advisor. Success depended on many interacting aspects, ranging from menu choices and cook staff to customer services and marketing. A few examples were given to demonstrate how experienced coaching sent quickly to stores having difficulties led to improvements in profitability.

Following all the manager reports, assistants brought in bottles of champagne, and all present drank a toast to the continued success of Peak Performance Poke. That evening, they would gather with all local employees as well as a number of international ones who flew in for a huge party to celebrate.

Kat and Vic went later that afternoon to the local coffee shop where Felipe used to work as a barista. It was their favorite, even without his talented latte creations. They perched on tall stools and looked out the large window at passing traffic and people. Both were reflective and nostalgic.

"Well, Kat, you've certainly done extremely well with your second business venture," said Vic.

"Not just mine, but ours," Kat replied. "You're a huge part of this success. I've learned so much about partnership and teamwork from you."

"With all the financial resources brought in by the business, you could afford to live the way you used to—world-class lifestyle, you called it," Vic remarked with a grin.

Kat threw back her head and laughed.

"Yeah, guess I could . . . but in truth, I don't want to go back. Frank and I are really happy living in Dad's home. It's comfortable and unpressured. And, Sky loves the neighborhood, even though he's not home much now since he went off to university."

"You and Frank have been married how long? Is it already two years? Wow, how time flies," Vic said, trailing off.

"Sure does," Kat agreed. "It's hard to believe Sky has already been going to university for nearly two years, too. He'll graduate this spring."

"Is he going to pursue a professional baseball career? He's been such a star with the university team, and I know recruiters have been after him."

"He hasn't made that decision yet, but I think he's leaning toward it," said Kat. "But if he decides on a business career, he has a good educational foundation. My long-term dream is that someday Sky will take over my part of the poke restaurant franchise. Family tradition and all, you know."

The women laughed and finished their lattes while looking back over their rocketing path to business success. By now, Vic was well-steeped in the models and principles that Vince had taught Kat—the same ones they both implemented in their daily operations of the business. Vic fully understood that these were not only for career and business, but were powerful guides to living a championship life in every aspect.

"Here's to bringing the business into the Championship Season," Vic said, raising her latte cup. Kat clinked cups and smiled.

"And here's to maintaining peak performance for our team and business into the foreseeable future," Kat replied.

"What do you think were the most important of your dad's lessons in getting your life back on track?" Vic asked. Only her close relationship with Kat permitted her to ask such a personally significant question.

Kat spent a few minutes in reflection. She knew that each and every model and principle had importance and contributed to the changes in her life.

The Championship Hour helped her begin every day on the right track. Principles of Teamwork kept her interacting effectively with both co-workers and family. She was constantly aware of how important Being Present was; how valuable the Gift of Now was in all relationships. Being Present in each moment also allowed her to become the observer and kept her aware of options for behaviors. When she needed to accomplish an action or task, Getting into the Zone was a highly effective skill. When she needed to make changes or take challenging actions, she relied on the Inner Game, understanding that high-level performance was an Inside-Out Process; she began with what was inside to affect outside actions. She understood that Giving up your Power was a choice; no one could take it away unless you gave it to them.

Vince's LSGT (Learn-Study-Grow-Train) model was among the most powerful tools for making change. Whenever she encountered a challenge or faced a failure, she used it to analyze what happened, learn, and grow from it, and entrain new behaviors. Sometimes change required applying the 180-Degree Mindset principle so she could move in opposite directions. Another key approach to change was using the Power of Gratitude, which shifted her internal compass away from anger and resentment to acceptance and appreciation.

When she had delved into truly understanding the 8 Forms of Wealth, it transformed her life. She came to realize that her definitions of success and wealth had been narrowly focused on Career/Business and Finances, and other aspects of her life were languishing. When she made the choice to seek wealth in all areas—Family, Relationships, Health and Fitness, Lifestyle, Personal Development, Spirituality—her happiness and fulfillment made leaps forward. She had been able to apply the 9-Point System for Success in every area and felt her overall satisfaction greatly improved. Part of this meant she was constantly Fighting the Enemy, those circumstances and habits that would undermine success. She used the Sunday Game Sheet to make weekly assessments of how she was doing in all the aspects of life, whichever might be uppermost at a given time.

As an overview, she used the 4 Seasons to a Championship Life to follow the long-term trajectory. It helped to understand which season was occurring since she could better decide on areas that needed focus, and which tools were appropriate.

But which was the key?

"The most important. . ." Kat smiled at Vic, her heart filled with affection for her long-term friend who had always stood beside her and offered honest feedback. "Naturally,

I'd say that all of them are important. But if I were to say which was absolutely essential for making changes, I'd have to choose The Observer. You must be able to stand back and watch yourself with clear eyes. This is the foundation of self-awareness, and change isn't possible unless you can identify your state of being. When you do this, you have the ability to change your state, because that power of choice is always within you. Then you enter a state of true self-mastery. Becoming The Observer empowers you to enter this awareness moment-to-moment. You have more opportunity for choice and change.

"By embracing The Observer, I've become a better person and am living a more balanced life. I've found my way to the fulfillment and satisfaction of my dreams."

"Well said!" Vic observed with enthusiasm. "And, to make a point: you didn't just repeat your previous business success. You've become 100 times more successful in your career and business."

"Most of all, I'm finally truly happy with my life," Kat concluded.

A NOTE
FROM THE AUTHOR

In 1993, I had just won my second World Championship in Toronto with the Blue Jays. From the outside, it probably looked like I was on top of the world. I mean, really—here was this young guy in his 20s making millions of dollars on the back-to-back world championship team. What could possibly go wrong?

Well, there was one massive problem. When I looked at myself in the mirror, I didn't like the person staring back at me. In fact, I hated him. I hated that he would explode anytime he couldn't control a situation. I hated that he was the one, in my mind, responsible for my brother's death.

From the time I left the hospital room where my little brother passed, I dealt with three emotions.

The first was to be expected: I was devastated that he was gone. But I was also angry. I was angry at the world, and I was angry at God. Underneath all that anger, I felt guilt. I felt guilty that it was my bone marrow that was rejected, which resulted in a coma and his eventual death.

I walked out of that hospital room with the weight of the world on my shoulders, and anytime I couldn't control a situation, the emotions came pouring out—primarily in the form of rage.

After the 1993 World Series, I was tired. I was tired of under-performing, not only in baseball but in my everyday life. I knew I could be a better player, and I knew that I wasn't responding well to life's situations. I was sick of being angry all the time and not understanding why. So, after a recommendation from one of my mentors, I dug deep. I reached out to a guy by the name of Harvey Dorfman. Harvey was the top psychologist and mindset coach inside Major League Baseball. He had helped other guys turn around their entire careers and was known as the *guru* for mindset and high performance, especially for pitchers.

Harvey knew all the players by name and had already figured out how their performance and mindset were connected before he ever talked to them in person. On our first phone call, he told me he had been waiting for me.

While I had reached out to Harvey after the 1993 season, I didn't actually meet with him until the spring of 1994. And *that's* when the idea of *The Observer* began. I met with him in a hotel room and immediately realized he had done some research on me beforehand. That guy nailed me from the get-go! Within the first hour, he pinpointed that I was still carrying around the baggage of blaming myself for my little brother's death, which had happened 12 years prior to that point.

As he began to ask me questions, it was very apparent to him that I was carrying around a tremendous amount of pain. He also knew, from experience, that this baggage would show up anytime I was pitching and lost control of the game—it was actually the pain that would fuel my emotional outburst, not the situation itself.

He asked me a very, very important question that day. We spent 12 hours together, and throughout those 12 hours, there was laughter and tears and high fives and hugs. . . but it was the question he asked that would have a lasting impact on my life for years to come.

"Todd, would you do it again?"

I knew he was talking about the bone marrow transplant.

"Man, Harvey, I would do it every minute. I would do it every minute of every hour of every day of every week. A month, a year, I don't care how long it is. I would do it over and over and over."

"Well, if you would do it all over again," he said, "it is time to let it go."

He was basically saying, "You've done everything you can, and you would do everything all over again, so you gotta shed the blame and welcome the forgiveness."

And so I went from blame to forgiveness in an instant. It was a powerful moment when I realized I'd done everything I possibly could have, and even though it wasn't good enough, it was all I could do.

That day, he told me something peculiar. He said, "Todd, if you would have said no, I would have told you to honor the defeat."

When you think about it, so many people are carrying around baggage. And the simple way to release that baggage is to learn the power of forgiveness. Whether you have to forgive someone else (or multiple people), or you have to forgive yourself, it is imperative to release that weight so it doesn't control you.

Think about Kat: she had to forgive herself for her marriage, for not spending enough time with her son, herself for not being there for her father, and for the way she was treating people—among many other things!

Before I left that day, he instructed me to do a seven-day challenge. In that seven-day challenge, it was my job to not react, and instead, to *record*. I was to record all my thoughts, emotions, and responses over a seven-day period. Instead of trying to control outcomes, what I was to focus on was controlling my *mind*.

That day, he said something that completely changed my life. You might remember it from Kat's story.

"People can take your body, but they can't take your mind unless you give it to them."

It was in that moment I realized that the blame, the pain, my emotional outbursts—it was all a result of giving away the power of my mind to, not only other teams in Major League Baseball, but to various situations in my life.

I'll never forget how it felt to leave that hotel room empowered to make a change. For the first time in my life, I had tools to help me. I left with the task of recording everything—from my thoughts to my emotions that corresponded—and the opportunity to see how I would respond to each situation I faced. So it began a habit of journaling; the beginning of me analyzing, reflecting, and observing the thoughts I had every single day, the emotions that were tied to those thoughts, and the responses I had the choice to make.

Thus began the journey of the observer—the choice that lies right between something happening and our response. The choice to become the observer. That's the exact place where these words become real: though they can take our body, they can't take our mind unless we give it to them.

Now, from that moment in the spring of 1994 until today, I've tapped into the power of the observer almost every single day. It's an incredible tool and resource that paves the way for explosive growth and high achievement.

Even though decades later, I've learned to become the observer, it's an ongoing battle of mastery. As we address and uncover the observer, we discover tools that lie in the toolbox—the same tools that Kat got to use and implement throughout her journey.

I think the main takeaway I want to leave you with here is that once you understand the observer and take the responsibility of becoming the observer, no failure will ever look the same in your life. Failure actually becomes something exciting, something to work on; a new challenge and a new way of growth. With this in mind, the responsibility to become the observer is really pursuing the best version of yourself.

Five years ago, when I was with my father as he fought multiple myeloma, I got to tell him how much he inspired me through his warrior-like mentality. I watched him fight cancer for 20 years, and it inspired me. Through that inspiration, it also registered that I've had the gift of coaches and mentors; the gift of incredible resources of gifted people to help me achieve great successes in my lifetime. In that same moment, it occurred to me that I hadn't passed that inspiration along.

So, for me, this book is my gift to you. It's my gift of experience to pass along to someone else who wants to climb higher mountains and grow as they take on bigger challenges—my message from the mess I've had to overcome.

As you've journeyed through this book and learned lessons from Kat, Vince, and Sky, I want to charge you to implement them in your own life. The gift of the observer is yours for the taking—you just have to commit to putting in the work.

ABOUT THE AUTHOR

I grew up around a majestic place called Yankee Stadium, where my father was an All-Star pitcher for the New York Yankees. Dad had great teammates like Mickey Mantle, Whitey Ford, Thurman Munson, and Yogi Berra as his first manager. Growing up in that environment inspired me to dream of following in Dad's footsteps and playing major league baseball. I had a goal, and I became obsessed with seeing it through. My mother and father were huge influences on my life; they believed in pursuing your dreams. I can still remember my Dad saying, "Whatever you decide to do, give it everything you have and be the best that you can possibly be."

LIFE AFTER BASEBALL

After baseball I went into the business world. I worked for a Wall Street firm for five years before launching my own investment fund. Once again, I was surrounded by incredible business talent. Soaking up everything I could and becoming better at what I was putting my effort into. Today, I'm building a global marketing business with some of the brightest entrepreneurs I have ever been around.

In life, baseball, and business I've experienced both failure and great success. I've learned from the best. I continue to learn and strive to get better every day. It is my desire to inspire you to dream again, with the imagination of a child—limitless. To guide you through the ups and downs of life. Yes, you will fall, but it's getting back up every time that counts.

DREAM BIG, SET BIG GOALS, AND GO FOR IT.

IT'S TIME TO AWAKEN THE CHAMPION THAT LIVES INSIDE YOU.

BECOMING
THE OBSERVER

To learn more about "Becoming the Observer," head over to the official website: ToddOfficial.com

UNLOCK AN UNLIMITED MINDSET
WITH THE INNER CIRCLE

If you're ready to finally make a change and build the life you truly want, Todd Stottlemyre's Inner Circle is your secret weapon to making it happen. You'll have access to trainings, resources, inspiration, and even monthly live Q&A's with Todd that will educate, motivate, and inspire you.

The Inner Circle is for people who are ready to start their transformation and be held accountable for their goals. If you're tired of feeling weighed down by the anchors in your life, today is the day you move forward!

TO LEARN MORE, VISIT: InnerCircle.ToddOfficial.com

OTHER WORKS BY TODD STOTTLEMYRE

When pursuing major league achievements, you are going to face extreme pressure. With a system in place to combat these pressures head-on, success is inevitable.

Pave the way to your success through this 9-part system influenced by peak performance coaches for elite athletes. By adopting this system for seizing your big opportunity, you're sure to stay ahead of the curve in your pursuit of excellence.

Available at your favorite store or online retailer as a book, audiobook, and eBook.

CPSIA information can be obtained
at www.ICGtesting.com
Printed in the USA
JSHW041339031220
9982JS00004B/4